High School Substitute Teacher's Guide: YOU CAN DO THIS!

Cherise Kelley

ISBN-13: 978-1479229642

ISBN-10: 1479229644

Table of Contents

DEDICATION

This teacher's guide is dedicated to all students, everywhere.

MY QUALIFICATIONS

"You're a high school substitute teacher?"

"Are you crazy?"

"We were so mean to them!"

These are common reactions when I tell people what I do, but I love substitute teaching at the high-school level.

My substitute-teaching career started at Alameda Unified School District in California, in 1989. I wasn't married yet, so those records are under my maiden name, Cherise Morris. I had just earned my BA in English from UC Berkeley. I planned to teach high-school English. I was looking for a way to support myself while I took my teacher-training classes and did my teaching internship (called "student teaching").

I took these "student teaching" graduate courses in secondary education at San Francisco State University (SF State). The secondary education department at SF State recommended me to the California Commission on Teacher Credentialing for two California teaching credentials: "Single Subject: English" and "Multiple Subjects for the Self Contained Classroom." Their multiple subjects recommendation was based on my testing in the

98th percentile on the National Teacher Examination (NTE) in General Knowledge. I got both of these teaching credentials in January of 1991.

However, I wrote to the education department at SF State anonymously once, to see what they would say about me, and they erroneously said that I had studied elementary education. I think this mistake happened because they put my file in their elementary education drawer after recommending me for the Multiple Subjects credential. Rest assured; I studied secondary educational methods and mentality. "Secondary education" is what they call middle school and high school, as opposed to elementary school.

These "student teaching" classes that I took at the graduate level in college are the source of much of the information in this book. Fifteen years of actual teaching experience has tempered the information, though. I got straight A's at SF State. However, I know that I have a better command of the art of teaching now than when those courses were fresh in my mind, more than twenty years ago. Then, I knew it in theory. Now, I know in practice. Let's go back to the story of my teaching career:

I was looking for a job to support me through graduate school when a friend told me:

"You have a BA now, so you can be a substitute teacher."

Frankly, being a substitute teacher had never occurred to me, before he said this. I'll wager there are not many people whose goal in life is to be substitute teachers. It's just not something little kids say when you ask them what they want to be when they grow up. Sure, some say, "a teacher," but I have not even heard one say, "a substitute teacher." I saw the wisdom in applying, though. I thought it would give me some good experience to put on job applications once I finished my student teaching and was looking for a full-time teaching position.

This friend helped me apply for substitute-teaching positions, answered my anxious questions, and generally helped me not only get the job, but also do well on the job. In writing this book, I hope to be for you the friend I was lucky enough to have when I started to work as a substitute teacher.

I started out as a "kindergarten through grade 12" substitute. I did that for years before I realized something: as a non-parent, I really don't know how to deal with a room full of kids younger than 14 years old. If they cry, I am pretty much done for. Little kids cry all the time! They also are not very comfortable with change. I was terrified the one day I subbed in kindergarten. I had five kindergarteners crying in my face and screaming,

"We have to do it this way! Yes we do! Yes we do!"

The next morning, I called the substitute coordinator and begged her,

“Please don't ever put me in the kindergarten room again!”

"No ankle biters, eh?" was her response!

I kept at it, just never in the kindergarten room again. Since then, I have substituted in two different states, for nine different school districts, in more than 100 different schools. Some were in affluent neighborhoods, but others were in the ghetto. Most were in cities, but some were in suburbs and urban areas. No matter where you live in the US, I think I have subbed in schools like those near you.

Here are the details of my teaching experience:

Alameda Unified School District, California, 1989 – 1990, K-12 Substitute Teacher, as Cherise Morris

San Francisco Unified School District, California, 1990 – 1991, K-12 Substitute Teacher; Student Teacher at Galileo High School; and summer school 1992 regular teacher, STEP (a summer school program for incoming high-school freshmen at-risk of dropping out of school), 9th grade language arts, as Cherise Morris

Fairfield-Suisun Unified School District, California, 1992/1993, High School English Teacher, as Cherise Morris

Rio Vista Unified School District, California, 1993/1994, High School English and English as a Second Language Teacher, as Cherise Morris

Poulsbo School District, Washington, 1994 – 1996, Substitute Teacher, grades 7-12, as Cherise Kelley

North Kitsap School District, Washington, 1994 – 1996, Substitute Teacher, grades 7-12, as Cherise Kelley

Central Kitsap School District, Washington, 1994 – 1996, Substitute Teacher, grades 7-12, as Cherise Kelley

Central Texas College satellite campus at Submarine Base

Bangor, Washington, 1994/1995, Basic Skills Instructor (I taught remedial reading for sailors whose command thought they would do better on their qualifications exams if their reading comprehension improved.), as Cherise Kelley

Arcadia Unified School District, California, Summer 1995, Summer School High School English Teacher, as Cherise Kelley (My husband was out to sea with the US Navy, so I stayed with my father and taught summer school at the high school where my father taught.)

Franklin Pierce School District, Washington, Summer 1996, Summer High School Math and English Teacher (The math was at the pre-algebra level. I am credentialed in math in Washington.)

Quillayute Valley School District, Washington, 1996/1997, High School Substitute Teacher (If you wonder about the spelling of Quileyute here, the valley is spelled the European way, while the reservation and tribe names are spelled the way the people themselves spell their name.)

I started as a math teacher at Forks Middle School, but that was a disaster. As I said earlier, I can make do as a short-term substitute at the middle-school level, but as a non-parent, I do not know how to deal long-term with students under the age of 14. I greatly enjoyed subbing the rest of the year at Forks High School. I chaperoned the 1997 Forks High School prom. When Twilight came out I could picture each location Stephenie Meyer described.

Escondido Union School District, California, 1997/1998, Substitute Teacher, grades 7 - 12

Apple Valley School District, California, 2008 – 2010, Substitute Teacher 7-12, mostly day-to-day with one long-term English assignment (3 months)

Colton School District, California, 2008 - 2009, Remedial Reading Teacher (REACH), grades 7 & 8

From 1997 through 2007, I worked for Farmers Insurance. I started as a temporary clerk in the billing department and worked my way up to senior claims representative. I have a strong understanding of the business world that we teachers are preparing students to enter.

Up until 2011, substitute teaching was something I fell back on between jobs.

I tried for years to get tenure as a regular high-school English teacher, but life happened. I fell in love and moved from California to Washington State, where my future husband was stationed in the US Navy. There were so many qualified Navy wives in that town that the waiting list for teaching positions was ten years long.

I got anxious about ever getting a full-time high-school English teaching job and made the mistake of accepting a middle-school math teaching position in Forks, WA. Jobs were even scarcer there, so when that contract was up we moved back to California, where my credentials had expired.

I was in school to get my California credentials back when I fell into a job at Farmers Insurance, where I kept getting promotions I couldn't turn down, until they let me go in

2007. I took the 12 quarter units I needed to get my credentials back and started substitute teaching and applying for full-time positions.

The real estate crash ruined the tax base of every school district in the country. Suddenly, teachers were being laid off everywhere and getting a position seemed impossible. Again, I made the mistake of accepting a middle school teaching position, this time in remedial reading. That lasted a year, and then I was looking again. We decided to move back to Washington State, where at least the cost of living is lower.

In 2011, after another year as a substitute, I realized that substitute teaching at the high-school level is my favorite job.

I get to hang out with teens all day. I just waltz in and deliver the lesson plan someone else prepared. I don't have to plan any lessons, grade any papers, or fill in any progress reports. I don't have to chaperone any games, plays or dances, but I can if I want. I can take a day off whenever I want. I get two months off for summer, two weeks off for Christmas, and a week off for Easter. I have the best part-time job in town. When people ask me what I do, I tell them "I'm a high-school substitute teacher, and I love it!"

I am happy as a substitute, but many of my friends got their permanent teaching positions because they shined as substitutes. My advice will help all three types of substitutes: those who are happy subbing, those who are subbing because they can't get work in their fields, and those who are subbing in order to get experience they can apply to a full-time teaching position.

If you have been through a teacher-training program at a university, some of the ideas in this book will be familiar to you. However, it is one thing to read the ideas in a college textbook, and quite another to read in my book how these ideas play out in real classrooms with real live students. I tell you about both types of experience in this book: good experience you should replicate, and bad experience to avoid if you can.

GETTING HIGH-SCHOOL SUBSTITUTE-TEACHING JOBS

Many people find substitute teaching a difficult, unrewarding job. For this reason, turnover is high in the substitute-teacher pool. If there are no openings in your school district right now, there probably will be soon. Check back in about a month.

The trick to keeping this job is to do it so well that you find it fun and rewarding. That has been the case for me, and I hope that by reading this book and going in prepared, it will be the case for you as well. I recommend that you read this whole book before you apply, and especially before your first day in the classroom. As with any other job, there are things you are not even aware that you don't know.

Substitute teaching opportunities are generally not advertised. Visit your local school district's website. You can find it in your favorite search engine by entering your city and state with the phrase "school district." Click on the "Employment" link and follow their substitute-teaching application process. This might be under the "Certificated" heading. Teachers, counselors, librarians, and principals are "certificated" employees, while secretaries, teacher's aids, bus drivers, custodians, gardeners, security officers, and cafeteria workers are "classified" employees.

"Classified" school district employees have substitutes, too, but this is outside my area of expertise.

I have only worked in school districts which kept classified substitute assignments separated from teacher substitute assignments. Some school districts list substitute jobs for teachers and classified employees together in the same computer system. This is nice for substitute teachers who are paid the same regardless if they take a teaching position or an aide position. It is not so nice for substitute teachers who think they will get $150 for a day in a teacher position, and then end up with $70 for a day in an aide position (depending on your district's pay structure).

School districts vary on pay and on what is allowed. This is because unions negotiate contracts with individual school districts on behalf of teachers and classified staff. Some school-district contracts don't even allow certificated employees to accept classified positions, not even for a day. Clarify this on the school district's website if you can, and with the substitute coordinator if the information is not on the website.

If there is a full-time aide position available and you like the pay, look before you leap. You might disqualify yourself for it if you become certified as a substitute for teachers.

Even if you don't meet all the qualifications listed on the school district's website, you still have a chance of getting hired

as a substitute for teachers.

In most states, school districts can get emergency teaching credentials for potential substitute teachers, if their need for substitutes is dire enough. It usually is dire enough. Most school districts require substitute teachers to have a bachelor's degree (in any subject), and this is the one criterion they are strict about. Not all school districts require substitutes to have a bachelor's degree, though, so look at each district's website closely.

On your application, list any and all experience you have working with teens: your own teenage children and their friends, your friends' teenage children, church youth groups, retail jobs where you worked alongside teens, coaching, tutoring, teens who babysit for you, and so on.

About a week after you apply online, call the school district after 9:30 but before noon.

I have substituted for nine different school districts now, and I had to follow up with every last one. I never would have been hired as a substitute teacher if I had just waited for them to call me after applying online. If you apply in summer, wait until school starts before you call.

When you call, ask to speak with the substitute coordinator. Her typical work day is 4 till noon. However, from 4 until 9:30 she is busy making sure all the day's absences are covered, so don't bother her before 9:30 except as she has directed.

Ask the substitute coordinator if she needs any teacher

substitutes right now, and if your application arrived in her in-box. If the substitute coordinator tells you she has enough substitute teachers right now, then wait about a month and try again, especially as it gets closer to Christmas or May. Those are the times of year when the most regular teachers are absent.

In a public school district, the substitute coordinator is the one who makes the hiring decision. The elected school board formalizes her decision at their next monthly meeting. When you go in to see the substitute coordinator, it might seem like she is just a clerk in the office. She starts work at 4, remember, so by the time you see her at 10, she might look a little haggard. She is on the computer and on the phone all morning. She might wear her hair in a ponytail and dress in jeans. Make no mistake, the substitute coordinator has the power to accept you or reject you. Impress her.

Dress as you would for a job interview.

Dress to impress when you go see the substitute coordinator as well as the first five times you have any reason to go to:

- The school district office
- A school board meeting
- Any school campus

You never know who you will meet while you are there. Your clothes and grooming might be the only indication they have of how professional you are. Do not blow this by looking like a student, or worse! Even after the first five times, always dress professionally.

Those of us who are over 40 look more like teachers without really trying. Being over 40 is actually an advantage for getting substitute teaching jobs (but not regular teaching jobs, not in the public schools. For those, districts tend to hire 23-year-olds, right out of college. I just know this by observing. I do not know why public school boards prefer to hire really young teachers, just that they do.) Dressing professionally can only help. I go into greater detail on this in the chapter on dressing like a teacher.

You will be judged by even the most casual encounters with everyone at the schools and at the district office, so be your professional self at all school-district properties, at all times, with everyone. You never know who might contribute to the decision to hire you or to recommend you for assignments or even will recommend you for regular teaching positions.

A woman in a position to hire college graduates once confided to me that she ruled out any who showed up in "less than professional attire" right off the bat:

"You would not believe how they show up: in shorts and T-shirts, drinking a drink from the local coffee shop!"

She went on to say she nodded politely as they gave her their resumes, and then tossed those same resumes as soon as these disrespectful applicants left her desk. She explained her office was near the beach, but she maintained that was no excuse for applicants to show up in less than professional attire.

These recent college graduates apparently did not consider a request to deliver their resume in person as a request for a job interview. Make no mistake: any request for you to come see a potential employer in person is a job interview. Dress codes for job interviews vary greatly by industry, but in education, college graduates are expected to dress professionally. If it is hot outside, then this can be slacks and a dress shirt, rather than the full-blown suit, but shorts and a T shirt are definitely a bad idea.

Unlike you, regular teachers often go about in jeans and T shirts.

Don't make the mistake I did and assume all the young people at a high school are students! Some of the regular teachers are only 23 years old. Unbeknownst to me, I once told one she was sitting in my chair!

"I'm sitting in your chair?"

"Yep, please move."

"You know, we teachers compare notes on substitutes. If we like you, we request that you come back."

"Ulp!"

Teachers do compare notes on substitutes. Having been a regular teacher, I can confirm this. Regular teachers have the power to make sure you work a lot, or not much at all. Treat everyone you meet on any school-district property as if they are interviewing you for a job. They probably are.

At the high-school level, this includes students. Even if

they are actually students and not teachers who look like students, you never know whose kids they are. Beyond that, high-school students are old enough to have influence on their own. I think this is what many substitutes find so intimidating about subbing at the high-school level:

You cannot treat high-school students like children.

I tell you oodles more about this in the chapters on the actual teaching and how to keep students from wrecking the room and other horrors.

It may take several meetings with the substitute coordinator before you are hired on as a substitute teacher.

Get whatever documentation she requests. Take CPR if necessary, and get TB clearance if she says you need to. Go pay a doctor cash for a routine physical exam, if needed. Go to the police department and get fingerprinted. All of this has been required at various school districts I have subbed for. She is not pulling your leg on these requirements.

You might be scheduled for a formal job interview. If you are, this is a good sign they are going to hire you. Remember, there are many substitute teachers in the school district, not just one, so they hire a lot of people to put on the list. Handle this as you would any job interview: dress well, get a lot of sleep the night before, and prepare answers to interview questions they are likely to ask. If you carefully and thoughtfully read this book, then you will be prepared for their questions.

Being hired on as a substitute by the school district is only the first step.

The next step is getting actual substitute-teaching assignments. You do this by schmoozing.

In some high schools, the school office lady is the one who decides which substitute teachers the system will call with assignments. Before there were computers, she would call all the substitutes directly. Many older teachers are used to this, and so they call the office lady and let her be the one to put the assignments into the computer. She probably has a list of substitutes with their computer system ID numbers and phone numbers and areas of expertise.

Schmooze up the office ladies in all the high schools where you hope to substitute teach. Give them your business card or at least make sure they have your name, system ID, and phone number. I have written much more on this in the chapter on making friends with school office staff.

As I touched on just now, have business cards printed up, once you get signed on as a substitute teacher. Hand a business card to each adult you meet at any school-district property. At minimum, your business card should have your name, your substitute teacher ID number for each school district you work for, your email address, and your phone number.

My business card also has a smiling picture of me in professional attire, my major and university (BA English, UC Berkeley), my website (http://www.facebook.com/CheriseKelleyWriter), and a blurb on how I am a writer, editor and essay grader for hire.

I paper-clip my business card to the note I leave for each regular teacher to tell about how the day went. There is much more on this in the chapter on leaving a note for the regular teacher. I have been requested for more repeat substitute assignments because of these cards than for any other reason, according to the feedback I get from regular teachers. If you follow the rest of the advice in this book, your notes to regular teachers will always be professional, too.

I order my business cards online through http://www.vistaprint.com/. I'm not getting any kickback from them. They are just the least-expensive professional outfit I have found. I can get 250 cards with my picture on them and all my info printed in a custom font – delivered to my mailbox in a week or less – all for less than $15.

Business cards cost even less if you don't put your picture on them, but I like how easy my picture makes it for regular teachers to match my name with my face. Most teachers recognize my face because they have seen me in the halls or in the teacher's lounge on days when I subbed for another teacher. Leaving teachers I substitute for a business card with my picture on it increases the chance they will recognize me and request me to substitute again.

If you want to work every day, then apply at every school district in your area.

The friend who first told me all about subbing worked for three school districts, and said he worked pretty much every day. In a rural area you might only live close enough to one school district. In the city, some substitutes work for six or more school districts. So that they understand you won't always be available at the last minute, tell each school district that you work for other districts. Keep two things in mind, though:

1) You should be able to get to any high school in these school districts at an hour's notice. In the winter months when it is icy on the city streets, I find taking the bus more convenient than driving.

2) The more often you substitute, the sooner you will burn out and start to hate subbing. I give suggestions to help this situation in the chapter on avoiding substitute-teacher burnout.

Getting a substitute-teaching job is actually the easiest part, even in today's economy.

As I said, many people find this job difficult and unrewarding, so turnover is high. There are many job openings for substitute teachers. If there isn't an opening right now, there probably will be soon.

Doing the job well so that you enjoy it and keep it is the subject of the rest of this book.

I recommend that you read this whole book before you

show up at the school-district office and ask to speak with the substitute coordinator, let alone before you accept your first substitute-teaching assignment and enter the classroom as a substitute teacher. I have included everything I wish I had known before my first day as a substitute teacher. Coincidentally, all this information helps you answer job-interview questions, as well.

DRESSING LIKE A TEACHER

Sadly but truly, teenage students are judgmental. They will make up their minds on how well they need to listen to you based on what you are wearing. Be yourself. Do not wear anything that makes you uncomfortable. That said, do set yourself apart as an adult. Do not try to be hip or cool and fit in with the students. They have friends. They need a great substitute teacher.

When you are young, dressing like a teacher means dressing as if you were over 40. Borrow some of your parents' clothes or have them go shopping with you. If you have hip parents like I do, then take your grandma or your boring aunt (or uncle, for the guys) shopping with you. Yes, an older friend will do, just get input from someone who will help you dress older, a generation or two prior to yours. If you are close in age to the students, then you probably like the same styles they like. If you shop without the guidance of someone from an older generation, then you run the risk of looking like you are trying to fit in with the students, even if you are trying not to.

It isn't just about what you wear, either.

Do not give the students any reason to doubt your competence. Be well-groomed. We older folks most often are the ones who get lazy on this count, and it is a big mistake to get lazy with your grooming. Shower or bathe every day, and wash your whole body with soap, even if you get up late and have to rush out the door. Nothing feels so good as a shower, or so bad as not having had one. Wash your hair at least every other day. Use dandruff shampoo if you have flakes. Brush or comb your hair before you show up on any school-district property. Brush your teeth before you leave the house. Put on antiperspirant.

If you are shaking your head and saying this is obvious, good for you. Just wait until you see a substitute who shows up with stringy uncombed hair and then you hear him or her complain about how kids today won't listen. You will have arrived. If the person otherwise seems to be a responsible adult who would make a great substitute, then loan them your copy of this book. If they read it, that might make the difference between them being an effective substitute who stays in this job, or someone who finds the job too challenging and leaves it right away. Back to you:

Do not wear anything that is flashy, silly, sexy, tight, or outdated.

This is the single most important piece of advice in this book, so I am going to repeat it at least three times (but only in this chapter, so don't freak out): Do not wear anything that is flashy, silly, sexy, tight, or outdated. I want there to be no question in your mind about this, so here is what I mean:

Flashy

Flashy includes but is not limited to: metallic fabrics; expensive or designer clothes, accessories or shoes; hats of any kind; neon colors; big clunky watches; expensive jewelry; long or fake or decorated fingernails; and extreme make-up.

Usually, people dress flashy because they want others to think they are rich. If you are a substitute teacher, no one is going to think you are rich. It is ridiculous to try and look like a rich substitute teacher. Why ask to be ridiculed?

Silly

Silly includes but is not limited to: cartoon characters, big flowers or big designs of any kind, floppy hats, clothes or shoes that are too big or that sag, trendy items, and items that appeal to very young children, but are silly either to high-school students or to adults. Trendy items may not be silly to the students, but they probably are to the other adults at the school. Besides, you are trying not to fit in with the students, remember.

People who dress silly were generally class clowns or drama types in school. They like to get attention with their clothing. Unfortunately, getting attention with clothing is not conducive to being seen as an adult, and especially not an authoritative adult. Silly might work at the elementary school level, but high-school students won't take you seriously if you wear silly things, so don't.

Sexy

Sexy, well, you know what that includes. Don't dress sexy

to work as any kind of teacher. Just don't. Please. This means no skinny jeans on any school-district properties.

Please see the chapter on not setting a bad example for more on this. I wear skinny jeans on the weekend, but even in my single days I didn't go crazy with my evening wear. You never know who you are going to see when you are off work and out and about town. Keep that in mind, and you should be fine.

Tight

Tight clothes are the norm for kids and people in their early twenties. This goes back to the sexy thing again. The pants that you wear for substitute teaching need to be trouser cut, not skinny cut or flare-legged. The point of trouser-cut pants is they hide your figure, rather than showing it off. They make you less of a sex object and more businesslike.

Trouser-cut pants have pockets in the side seams. They fit snug at the waist, but they hang loose from the seat to the hem. They should be long enough that they rest on your shoes in the front, but not so long that they touch the floor in the back.

If you have only ever worn jeans, then trouser-cut pants are going to feel weird to you. Go to a department store and look at the trouser-cut pants. Try them on to see how they are supposed to fit, even if you later buy your substitute-teaching clothes at thrift stores. I give advice on how to shop for inexpensive clothing later in this chapter.

Outdated

Outdated clothing includes anything that is no longer fashionable. Most items of fashion, or "trendy" items, are only timely for a season, and then they become "so last year." A substitute teacher cannot afford to be fashionable. Classic styles of clothing never go out of fashion, though. Buy classic styles instead of fashionable styles so that you won't be outdated. Classic styles are the types of clothes that are the same in all movies, regardless of the year the movie portrays or the year it was made. Classic styles include preppy and business attire.

Preppy Style

Preppy dress style gets me the most cooperation and respect from students and staff when I substitute in most academic subjects — math, history, English, science, foreign language. By "preppy," I mean the way college professors dress in TV shows and movies:

- Argyle sweater
- Oxford-cloth dress shirt with button-down collar
- Short-sleeved Oxford-cloth dress shirt in warm weather
- Textured wool pants or skirt
- Textured wool sport coat in cold weather
- Loafers with ankle socks (even with a skirt)
- Tortoise-shell eyeglasses

- Necktie for men, one open button for women

You can probably get away with washable synthetic fabrics that look like wool. Just do some comparative shopping so that you get good synthetics that really look good. Go to an upscale store and look at wool garments. Feel them to see how they handle. Then, look at garments made of synthetic fabric that is supposed to look and feel like wool. Only choose synthetics that really do look and feel like wool and are washable. Check tags to make sure synthetic garments are washable. If they have to be dry cleaned, then you might as well get wool. Go with natural colors, rather than bright colors. Remember, nothing flashy.

Preppy attire does not mean you dress like a nerd. Do not wear a bow tie. Do not tape up your eyeglasses like nerds do in movies. It doesn't mean you dress like a slut, either. Do not wear a "skort" or a mini skirt, even if it claims to be preppy. Skirt length should be at or below the knee. If you sit down in a skirt that does not fall below the knee, make sure and cross your legs.

Business Attire

Business attire – suit and tie – probably works just as well as dressing preppy. My dad taught high-school history for 30 years. He won many awards, both as a teacher and as a Constitutional debate coach, and he always wore a suit and tie to school.

Wool is best for suits, but you can get washable separates that look like they are wool. Be careful to choose conservative cuts and colors. Remember, nothing flashy or sexy. Solids work best, rather than patterns.

A caveat with business attire is that some of it that is made for women is just too downright sexy to be worn while teaching. Pants need to be trouser-cut and loose, not tight. Do not wear a "skort" or a mini skirt, even if it claims to be business attire. Skirt length should be at or below the knee. If you sit down in a skirt that does not fall below the knee, make sure and cross your legs.

Business Casual

The two high schools where I currently substitute have extremely casual dress codes. Almost all the teachers wear jeans every day. The first five times I came to both campuses, I wore a skirted suit and nylons. The rest of that school year, I wore preppy attire. The next school year, I started wearing business casual attire.

For one thing, I lost 90 pounds that second year. None of those skirted suits fit anymore. I needed "new" clothes every month, as I got smaller and smaller. Everyone already knew me by sight and many by name, so the "first impression" time was good and over. I now wear business casual attire to substitute, and this is what it looks like:

- Trouser-cut pants: These can be cotton or even corduroys, but not denim of any color.
- Loose-fitting shirt or sweater that is not a T shirt
- Jacket that is not a jean jacket or a logo jacket

No matter which style you choose, aim to look like you mean business.

Dark colors make you look more businesslike than pastels — except on Southern women aged 35+ in the South, according to John T. Molloy's research into such matters (John T. Molloy, *The Woman's Dress for Success Book* [New York: Warner Books, Inc., 1977], 137). In warm weather you can skip the jacket and just wear slacks and a business shirt. Women can wear dresses, but make sure they are businesslike and modest, which means they hide your figure rather than enhancing it.

Pockets are a prime consideration when shopping for teaching clothes.

The pockets you use must be in your trousers or your skirt, in case you take your jacket off. See the chapter on arriving at the school for the list of what I bring to school with me. Women's clothes don't usually have enough pockets.

I carry an insulated lunch bag that is black and businesslike and that has compartments where I can separate pens and stuff from the food area. I got it at Walmart for less than $10, in the sporting goods department.

I used to wear a fanny pack, and unfortunately some of my students will tell you I wore one long after they became outdated. Once they started to tease me about it, I had to stick with it, just so they couldn't get the better of me. It was a long school year. Learn from my mistake; don't wear anything outdated!

Wear sensible shoes.

For guys, shoes are usually not an issue. I am speaking to the ladies here. Wear shoes that don't hurt your feet.

I wear loafers every day I substitute, even on days when I wear a dress. Loafers are expected with the preppy clothing I like to wear for subbing, so no one even comments about my loafers. I have several pair of loafers in different colors so that I can match my outfits and not wear the same pair two days in a row. I get the kind with rubber soles, so they are as comfortable as sneakers. Loafers aren't expensive, either. I get them at Walmart, Target, or Payless Shoe Source for less than $10 a pair.

I know it is customary to wear high-heeled pumps with business attire. Don't wear high heels for any kind of teaching. Why not? Three reasons:

1) You are on your feet all day. Your feet and ankles will thank you for wearing sensible walking shoes with rubber soles. If you think you can be effective at any kind of teaching without walking around the room constantly, then you are delusional. Get used to the idea that you will be on your feet all day. I tell you more about the strategy of "classroom management by walking around the room" in the chapters on the actual teaching and how to keep the students from wrecking the room and other horrors.

2) High heels are too sexy for a teacher to wear. If you are shaking your head and thinking I am stuck in the 1940s, well, I wasn't even born until the 1960s. More importantly, though, I believe the idea that women

should look sexy no matter what they are doing is put into society by men in order to keep women in subservient roles. I am going to invoke John T. Molloy's research again here to back me up. If you don't want to take my word on this, then read Molloy's book *The Woman's Dress for Success Book* and digest his extensive research: Break out of the mold of the sexy woman. Become the effective woman instead, at work.

3) You might be called on to period substitute for a physical education (PE) teacher, or one of the math teacher's classes might be a PE class. Wear soles that won't mark up the gymnasium floor.

That said, don't wear sneakers for substitute teaching, either. Wear shoes that look professional, but that walk like sneakers.

See-Through Fabric

Obviously, no teacher in his or her right mind would wear see-through clothing to school, right? I cannot tell you how many times I have seen teachers, especially female teachers, wearing see-through clothing at school! Too many times, they were wearing blouses so sheer you could see their bras underneath! Some of their pants were so sheer you could see their underwear!

Scandalous!

Just plain wrong.

I choose to believe these teachers were not aware their clothes were see-through. Check this carefully. Before you even take an item of clothing off the rack to consider trying it on, put something bright, such as the tag, behind the fabric. If you can see the tag through the fabric, don't even take that item of clothing off the rack. It is see-through.

In these tough economic times, more and more clothing companies are trying to save money by making the fabric so thin you can see through it. More than half the brand-new clothing items I tested this way at a local store, I couldn't even try on because the fabric was so thin you could see through it. Buyer, beware!

Gray Hair

In most other professions, gray hair is a liability. Teachers look best with gray hair. It lends us authority. I started going gray when I was 36, and unfortunately I started to dye my hair then. If I had it to do over, I would let my hair go gray. If I had shorter hair I would cut off all the dye. In my forties, my compromise was I didn't dye my bangs. Now at almost 50, I look ancient to high-schoolers regardless, so I just dye it all. I wear my long hair in either a bun or a low pony tail.

Resist the temptation to fit in with the students.

Many new teachers find it tempting to follow the students' fashion trends and try to make them think we are "cool." Resist this temptation, and not just in the area of fashion. Again, students have cool friends. They need you to be someone they can look up to as a mature adult. Someone like you has to step in and tell students to get back to work. They take this much more readily when you are dressed as an adult (and otherwise behave like an adult).

Where I currently substitute, in winter all the high-school girls wear skinny jeans tucked into their snow boots. It looks so cute! Now that I once again look OK in skinny jeans, my first impulse was to go get some snow boots to tuck them into and show up subbing like that. Whoa. Can you tell me three reasons I should not do this? 1) Nothing sexy. 2) Nothing tight. 3) Avoid the temptation to fit in with the students. I still might dress this way on the weekend, but I will not show up to teach dressed the way the students dress. At school, if I wear snow boots they will be under my trouser-cut pants.

Fresh out of college, I had to stick to wool for pants or skirts and wear eyeglasses, Oxford shirt, and a sweater vest, or I didn't get any respect. Now that I am over 40, I can cheat and wear cotton slacks (such as Dockers). I find cotton more comfortable, and of course I can throw it in the washing machine. Wool slacks and skirts need to be dry cleaned, so I use them only for first impressions. You can get away with washable fabrics that look like wool if you shop for them carefully.

On Fridays, I even wear loose-fitting jeans and a school sweatshirt, along with all the other staff. If I were under 40, I would not participate in sweatshirt Fridays. As it is, I don't participate in spirit week or Halloween costume days. Again, if I were under 40, then I would dress for business or wear preppy attire every day.

If you are on a strict clothing budget:

If you are on a strict clothing budget and have nothing appropriate to wear (or if what you have to wear is really nice and you want to save it for job interviews in your "real" field), then you can find inexpensive preppy clothing or business attire at thrift stores.

Thrift stores dry clean all their clothing before you have to touch it, so don't freak out. You won't come into contact with anyone's bodily fluids by trying on clothes they wore. The clothes are all clean and dry in the store. They do not stink. I have talked with people who actually thought thrift stores were like that, if you are laughing right now! Sometimes, a thrift store will even have brand-new clothing with the tags still on it.

Look at all the clothing in a thrift store, even the stuff for kids and people of the opposite sex, not just other sizes in stuff for your same sex — but look at that, too. Customers often put clothing in the wrong section after trying it on. Thrift stores are mostly staffed by volunteers, and not as heavily staffed as regular stores. The workers don't have as much time to put stuff away correctly, and they aren't as experienced with putting stuff away correctly.

Many thrift stores don't have fitting rooms, so the first time you visit a particular thrift store, wear something you can try clothes on either over or under. For example, you could try pants on under a maxi dress if you are female, or over tight swim shorts if you are male. You could try shirts on over a tank top. I never buy used shoes, but Walmart, Target and Payless Shoe Source all seem to sell loafers year round.

Did you notice I said, "the first time you visit a particular thrift store"? Yeah. The bad news about thrift stores is they only have what people have donated. They don't necessarily have what you are looking for, right now. You might have to shop all day, at four different thrift stores, just to find one substitute-teaching outfit. There is good news, though. These stores constantly get more donations.

Keep going back into your local thrift stores every few days until you have five substitute-teaching outfits. That way, you can be happy if you work every day in a week, and you will have the weekend to get it all clean and ready again for the next week.

Estate sales, garage sales and classified ads are more places you can buy inexpensive used clothes. I don't have much experience with these because their ads rarely mention what size the clothes are.

Some classes require special clothing consideration:

Physical Education (PE)

Wear a jacketed sweat suit over gym clothes. Don't forget a visor and sun screen in case you will be outside. Wear the kind of gym shoes that won't scuff the gym floor. Bring a whistle on a cord you can wear around your neck. Put long hair in a ponytail. Bring a clip board for taking attendance that you later transfer to the computer.

Art / Shop

Dress like an adult, but in older clothes that you don't mind getting stained. Loose-fitting jeans that you don't care about too much are actually a good choice for these classes. Don't wear a tie. It might hang down into a student's artwork and get dirty - or it might get caught in some machine and strangle you. Wear long hair up or tied back, for the same reasons.

Special Ed / Resource

Dress preppy or for business, but do not wear anything students could grab onto and hurt you:

- No tie
- No earrings
- No necklaces
- Wear long hair up tight.

Do not wear anything that is flashy, silly, sexy, tight, or outdated.

OK? If you get nothing else from this book, at least get that right. Substitute teachers have it difficult enough without dressing like class clowns, fools, or sluts.

Even if you are single and there is this school employee who is single and you really think you could hit it off, do not wear anything remotely sexy to school or to any work-related event. If you two are meant for each other, then you should get to know each other as "real people" first anyway, instead of as sex objects.

GETTING YOUR SUBSTITUTE-TEACHING LICENSE

Under the US Constitution, each state regulates education as it sees fit. For this reason, each state has its own Department of Education. Each state licenses its own teachers according to its own requirements. Some states license teachers; others credential them. Both terms have the same meaning.

If you need to take any classes to get your substitute-teaching credential, they will be offered online. Teachers constantly have to take classes to keep their licenses up to date, and everyone knows they are teaching classes during school hours.

If you are credentialed to teach out of state or in another country, some states accept that and apply it to their state's requirements. Not all states do this, but it doesn't hurt to ask. Be sure to ask as soon as possible, because it can take months to get paperwork through.

Many school districts are in such need of substitute teachers that they will appeal to their state's Department of Education on your behalf and get you an emergency teaching credential. If a school district is doing this for you, go ahead and skip this chapter.

If you are a veteran, "Troops to Teachers" might help you get a teaching license:

http://www.proudtoserveagain.com/

If your spouse is in the military, the Military Spouse Career Advancement Accounts (MyCAA) might help you to become certificated for substitute teaching:

http://www.education4military.com/military-spouse-career-advancement-accounts.asp

In case you don't have any such luck, here are the titles of the Web pages where each of the teacher-licensing branches of all 50 US state departments of education list their teacher licensing procedures. I list these to help you apply directly with your state.

Alabama Teacher Certification

Alaska Teacher Certification

Arizona Transition to Teaching

Arkansas Educator Licensure

California Commission on Teacher Credentialing

Colorado Educator Licensing

Connecticut Educator Certification System

Delaware Teacher Licensure/Certification Initial Application Instructions

Florida Educator Certification

Georgia Educator Certification

Hawaii Teacher Standards Board

Idaho Teacher Certification

Illinois Educator Certification

Indiana Prospective Educators

Iowa Board of Educational Examiners

Kansas Teacher Education and Licensure

Kentucky Education Professional Standards Board

Louisiana Become a Certified Teacher

Maine Certification and Professional Development

Maryland Department of Education, Certification Division

Massachusetts Becoming an Educator

Michigan About Teacher Certification

Minnesota Educator Excellence

Mississippi Educator Licensure

Missouri Educator Certification

Montana Educator Licensure

Nebraska Teacher Certification

Nevada Teachers Licensing

New Hampshire Certification / Bureau of Credentialing

New Jersey Overview to Certification

New Mexico Public Education Department Educators

New York Teacher Certification

North Carolina Professional Educator's Licensure

North Dakota Credential Application Forms

Ohio Educator Licensure Applications

Oklahoma Teacher Certification

Oregon Teachers, Laws & Licensure

Pennsylvania Teacher Certification

Rhode Island Educator Certification

South Carolina Educator Certification

South Dakota Certification Process

Tennessee Teacher Licensing

Texas Educator Certification

Utah Teaching and Learning Licensing

Vermont Educator Licensing

Virginia Teaching Licensure

Washington Teacher Certification

West Virginia Educator Certification

Wisconsin Teacher Licensing Information

Wyoming Professional Teaching Standards Board

THINGS TO GET FROM THE SUBSTITUTE COORDINATOR

Once you get hired on as a substitute teacher with a school district, that district's substitute coordinator will probably have you come see her for an orientation meeting. If this is one of the first five times you have met her, then dress as if you were going to a job interview. You just might be, even if that is not what she calls it.

Be sure and get some things from the substitute coordinator that will greatly reduce your anxiety and help you do your job better. She should give you or show you where to find on the Internet:

- Procedures for using the online substitute teacher assignment system
- Your substitute teacher ID number that teachers can use to request you in the system (so you can put it on the business cards you are going to order as soon as you leave her office)
- ID badge
- Parking pass and parking locations and policies for each school where you will be substitute teaching

- ➢ Log-in, password, instructions for and policies governing all school-district software you will be using. At the district where I currently work, we are only to be on the computer doing things for the class we are currently teaching. We are not to plan for the next class during the current class (or surf around for fun). Read these policies and adhere to them, or you could lose your job over something as trivial as reading a fashion article online.

For each high school in the district, also get:

- ➢ address
- ➢ phone number
- ➢ school office opening time
- ➢ bell schedule

Impress your substitute coordinator, and stay on her good side. You don't really have an immediate supervisor, as a substitute teacher. The substitute coordinator is the closest thing you get. She is the one who makes sure you work at least once in a while. She is the one who keeps your human resources file up to date.

What you won't get from the substitute coordinator is a performance review or a job recommendation.

The substitute coordinator does not observe your performance in the classroom, and in most school cultures that is required in order to recommend you. In case you decide substitute teaching is not your favorite job and you want to get something else, or in case you move to a new city and need to get a substitute-teaching job there, you have to get your job recommendations from whoever will give them.

When you are a new substitute teacher, you never know which regular teacher or school administrator might turn out to be the one you need to ask for a letter of recommendation. It is important to impress (and stay on good terms with) every teacher in all the buildings of every school district where you substitute teach.

So far as feedback on how well you are doing your job as a substitute, for most of us that only comes in the form of more or fewer substitute-teaching assignments.

If you are doing a good job, then teachers request you and tell other teachers about you. You get requested often to come substitute, if your performance is good. If you are not doing a very good job, then your name moves to the bottom of the list and you only get called in to substitute on days when a lot of teachers are out and they need all the substitutes on the list to come in.

Some school districts enable teachers to post performance evaluations for substitutes who were in their classrooms on the online substitute assignment system. If you substitute in one of these school districts, you might be able to see these evaluations, but you might not. Some districts hide these evaluations from the substitutes themselves and just make them visible for other regular teachers to see. The reasoning here is that the other regular teachers could use this information when they are selecting which substitute they want to request to cover their next absence.

If job performance feedback is important to you, then ask the substitute coordinator if her district allows regular teachers to post feedback that the substitutes can see. She might fill you in on some other feedback system her district has in place that I have not heard about. In my experience, feedback is the exception, rather than the rule for substitute teachers. Even if you do receive feedback, still be on the lookout for teachers and administrators who observe you in the classroom and who would be willing to write letters of recommendation for you.

When I was a regular classroom teacher, I worked 70+ hours per week and never had time to give substitute teachers any feedback. I had been a substitute already, myself, and knew what it was like, but I truly did not have time to even request who subbed in my classes, let alone give them any feedback.

Regular teachers have to plan lessons, grade papers, meet with parents, and fill out progress reports. They work more hours than most, on salary, with no overtime pay. Do not expect feedback from regular teachers.

You will get a letter from the substitute coordinator at the end of each school year.

If the letter is not from the substitute coordinator, it will be from the school board. It will look like either 1 or 2:

1) Your services have not been renewed for the next school year. This is bad. It is the same thing as being

fired. There is not much you can do except look for other work. You might be able to collect from your state's unemployment insurance with this letter, though. It wouldn't hurt to apply. Each state has its own policy on whether or not public school employees can collect unemployment insurance benefits.

2) You have "reasonable assurance" of work for next year. Would you like to return as a substitute next year? This is asking if you want them to continue offering you substitute assignments next year. Unless you definitely have another job, check the "Yes" box and send it back to them right away. This does not prevent you from being hired on as a regular teacher. It just lets them know you want to continue working for the school district next year.

The "reasonable assurance" phrase in that #2 letter is code for "No, school employees cannot collect unemployment insurance payments over the summer." Summers are lean times for substitute teachers, and what makes it even worse is teachers aren't absent the first few weeks of school. Substitute-teaching work doesn't pick up until school has been in session for a few weeks.

Worse still, most school districts pay at the end of October for work completed in September, and so on.

You get a check at the end of July for the work you did in June, and then you don't get another paycheck until the end of October. Three months without a paycheck is more than most people can last. See the chapters on avoiding substitute burnout and ideas for making money over the summer and during Christmas break.

When you get home from seeing the substitute coordinator:

Input all the high-school addresses into your GPS or phone ahead of time, to save you from panicking later.

Make several copies of the bell schedules. Post one for each school where you can check it before you leave for school in the morning. Place one in your substitute folder for each school.

See the chapter on arriving at the school.

MAXIMIZING YOUR SUBSTITUTE-TEACHER PAY

All the school districts where I have subbed have paid significantly more than I could have made at a retail job. I have made as much as $150 per day and as little as $80 per day for substitute teaching. Each public school district in the US has fixed amounts they pay for any given job, based on a published chart you can usually see on the school district's website. Some pay high and some pay low, usually depending on their area's property tax revenues.

Regular teachers get pay raises each year as their education and experience put them higher on the pay-scale chart. Some public school-districts pay certified substitute teachers more than those with just emergency credentials. I have heard there are districts that give substitutes a raise after so many years. Practices vary greatly from state to state and from school district to school district.

Most substitute teachers only get pay raises for long-term substitute-teaching assignments. In other words, most substitutes only make more money after they substitute a given number of consecutive days for the same regular teacher. Each public school-district makes its own rules regarding how many consecutive days equals a long-term substitute-teaching assignment. I have heard of the required number of days being 6, 11, 20, 30, or even 130.

Some school districts will avoid giving a substitute the long-term subbing pay raise by taking a substitute out of a classroom for a day and then putting her back in. Don't be shocked if this happens to you. Don't count your chickens before they are hatched. Instead, be grateful if it doesn't happen and you get the higher pay for being a long-term substitute. I write more about long-term substitute assignments in the chapter by that name.

Private schools need substitutes, too.

I do not have experience substituting at private schools, but I assume much of the information in this book will apply there. On average, private schools pay less than public schools. If you are substituting for the joy of it or for the teaching experience, or if you really need a job, then this might be acceptable to you. If it is, then you should contact each private school in your area. One plus that I have heard about private schools is their students are often better-behaved that at public schools. This is because parents are paying extra, beyond just taxes, and so the parents have extra motivation to make students behave at private schools.

There is little you can do to change the pay rate for substitute teachers. That is not what this chapter is about.

If your public school-district pays substitutes close to minimum wage and you are subbing for the money rather than for the experience or the joy, then you are not going to get much out of this chapter. I feel for you. This chapter does have advice that can help a little, though.

Generally, substitute teachers only get paid for hours that we actually work. Like most other part-time workers, we don't get sick days or vacation pay. Most of us don't get health insurance through our school district, but you can get health insurance directly from an insurance company, through an insurance agent, or through websites such as http://www.ehealthinsurance.com/.

Unlike regular classroom teachers, most substitute teachers don't get paid for jury duty. I usually just tell the court I don't get paid unless I actually work, and they usually excuse me from jury duty. Most people who work for school districts are ineligible for unemployment insurance over the summer or any other time school is not in session.

Teachers' unions have negotiated half-day minimum pay with most school districts.

Substitute teachers can join the union, but we don't have contracts; regular teachers do. For this reason, joining the union doesn't help substitutes as much as it helps regular teachers. We do mysteriously get some of the contracted hours that the unions have negotiated for the regular teachers, though. This is a good thing, although many substitutes, previously including me, mistakenly complain about it. Let me explain.

Substitute teachers benefit from half-day minimum pay in all the school districts where I have subbed. This means we get half a day's pay for showing up to an assignment, even if the school only needs us for one or two class periods. The down side that I complained about is that sometimes an administrator will cancel those assignments where the school only needs a substitute for one or two class periods. It makes sense for the administrator to do so. They can cover one or two class periods with regular teachers period-subbing on their preparation periods. It's lousy for the substitute who had an assignment a minute ago, but now does not, and got canceled too late to get another assignment. Oh well.

The downside I don't understand people complaining about is that the substitute coordinator expects us to stay at the school for the entire time we are being paid. This is what that looks like in the school district where I substitute right now:

Students are dismissed at 2:15, but contracted teachers

have to stay on campus until 2:45. Substitutes are also expected to stay until 2:45. At the elementary schools, they keep substitutes busy for that extra half hour, supervising students on the playground until their bus comes or their parents pick them up. At the high school, there is usually nothing for substitutes to do during that extra half hour after school lets out.

Many substitutes whine and groan about having to stay that extra half hour with nothing to do but read, chat, walk the halls, or play on their phones. Why complain, though? We are being paid to stay there until 2:45.

Another very important piece of advice I have for you, besides dress appropriately, is don't complain. Public school staff hear whining and complaining all day from the students. They have had it "up to here" with listening to people complain. Do not add more complaining to what they hear, or you may be sorry.

I have control over being ready to accept a substitute-teaching assignment when the phone rings in the morning.

Sometimes, I am blessed with a subbing assignment ahead of time, rather than an hour before I need to run out the door to head over to the school. Most of the time, this is because a regular teacher knew in advance that he would be absent. He used my business card to contact me and arrange for me to be there. Once we made this agreement, he assigned me on the computer.

Almost all school districts assign substitutes by computer. Most school districts allow each substitute to search online at home for future assignments. The first substitute who claims a posted assignment gets it. Also, I am good at what I do, so a lot of teachers I have subbed for in the past request me ahead of time. When they do this, the system calls me until I accept or decline the assignment.

However, regular teachers have many more sick days than they have discretionary days off. Understandably, most substitute assignment systems assume sick days will be scheduled at the last minute. After all, who knows ahead of time that they are going to be sick, right? So, most of these online assignment systems don't allow regular teachers to schedule sick days ahead of time. Teachers have to call in sick the morning of the absence.

For this reason, most of my substitute-teaching assignments come by phone any time from 5:30 in the morning to 5 minutes before I need to leave the house. However, it usually appears to me that the regular teacher did, indeed, know ahead of time that she was going to be sick. How else would she have known to leave substitute lesson plans on her desk?

Being ready to leave the house at 7 each morning even though that phone hasn't rung yet can mean the difference between:

1) Arriving when school starts and being paid for a whole day, and

2) Arriving an hour after school starts and missing an hour's pay. Those hours all add up.

So, every weekday evening I act as if I am going to be subbing the next day.

I plan for it. I anticipate getting that call.

I start thinking about tomorrow's lunch on my way home the day before, in case I need to stop at the market before the evening gets away from me. I make tomorrow's lunch just before I take my evening shower. If I don't end up substituting, then I just eat my packed lunch at home the next day.

I always have at least one outfit ready that is suitable for subbing. I check my clothing situation as soon as I get home and do laundry right then, if I need to. This is where washable synthetics or cotton really come in handy. It is impossible to get things dry cleaned the night before you need to wear them, but you can go to the laundromat the night before, if need be. I have been in that situation.

I shower with soap and wash my hair before I go to bed. I at least rinse off in the morning.

I make sure and go to bed by 10 every night. I don't read in bed. I go to bed at 10 and am asleep right away. If I don't get to sleep by 10, then I am miserable at school the next day.

I quit my caffeine intake by 2 every afternoon. Caffeine is active in my system for up to 8 hours, so I cannot have any after 2 and expect to go to sleep at 10. I stop all caffeine intake at 2, even on the weekends. This makes it much easier to get up in the morning on school days.

If you have trouble getting to sleep, then it may be that

caffeine is active in your system for this long, as well. Try quitting your caffeine intake 8 hours before you need to go to sleep. Remember this means not just coffee, but also most sodas. Most root beer and lemon-lime sodas are caffeine-free, but not all, so read labels.

I set my alarm for a few minutes before the earliest time the substitute assignment computer is allowed to call me.

I check the computer to see if I can grab any assignments before it calls anyone. Even if there aren't any assignments I can grab now, I might still get a call. The day is young. Teachers call in sick up to the minute before school starts. Sometimes they show up to class and feel too sick to stay. I have been called in to substitute the same day as late as 10 in the morning.

I have a good breakfast that does not include too much coffee. I have to watch my liquids before and during substitute assignments, as teachers are not supposed to leave students unattended in the classroom. I have written an entire chapter about this, later in the book.

For those assignments that come right before school starts, your substitute coordinators will be impressed (and you can avoid missing an hour's pay) if you are already up, showered, breakfasted, lunch packed and eager to go when they call you 5 minutes before you need to leave the house.

For assignments that come first thing in the morning, you work more days if you are awake when the phone rings! If you don't answer the phone, chances are the next substitute in the call rotation will, and you will miss out on a day you could have been working and making money.

One of the only perks of substitute teaching is you can take a day off whenever you want.

The school district won't pay you for time you are not working, but it is easy to take a day off. It doesn't matter why you want the day off. You don't have to explain to anyone that your kid has something going on at school or you want to attend a club meeting during business hours or you have a doctor's appointment. All you have to do is make yourself unavailable for subbing assignments that day in your school district's online substitute teacher assignment system. You can even cancel an assignment that you had already accepted. I wouldn't do that very often, but you can if you need to, like if you or someone in your family gets sick, for example.

Reasons I have made myself unavailable for substitute assignments vary.

I have had honorable reasons such as doctor and dentist appointments, but I have also had frivolous reasons such as wanting to stay up late in order to watch a movie or finish reading a novel. I only get asked why I am unavailable if I reject a job that is offered to me (which won't happen if I am unavailable), or if I had to cancel a substitute teaching job that was already assigned to me. I only cancel for illness or business reasons.

In the past, I have held other part-time jobs during a school year while I was also substituting. I did my best to make my second employer understand I could not work during school hours, but sometimes they needed me to cover for a full-time employee who was out for an extended period of time. This was no problem. I just went into the school district's online substitute assignment system and made myself unavailable for that period of time. You can read more on this in the chapter on Money-Making Ideas for Summer and Christmas breaks.

Important Caveats to taking days off whenever you want:

Some school districts require substitute teachers to work a certain number of days per month or per semester to remain active in the substitute teaching pool.

Be aware of any such requirements in every school district where you substitute. Ask the substitute coordinator about this. In a district that has a policy such as this, I would not make myself unavailable at all for silly reasons such as wanting to finish reading a novel. If you are sick or have to care for a sick family member, then of course take yourself off assignments.

Some school districts, schools, and substitute coordinators hate it when you reject a substitute assignment that you are offered.

Some substitute coordinators hate it so much when you reject an offered assignment that if you reject one too many assignments they will fire you.

My current substitute coordinator was nice enough to explain to us at orientation that she falls into this camp. She warned us that she hates it when substitutes reject assignments offered to us. She advised us to make ourselves unavailable for any days we were not going to accept assignments.

Not all substitute coordinators will tell you their preferences or even what their systems keep track of, though. With many, you won't know you have rejected or canceled too many assignments. You will just get a letter from the school board, saying your services are not being renewed for the next school year. For this reason, it is better if you make yourself unavailable for substitute assignment offers, rather than reject assignment offers that you receive or cancel assignments you have already accepted.

I have heard that some school districts configure their computerized substitute-teaching assignment systems to ask you for a reason for being unavailable. I feel this is none of their business unless I am trying to collect unemployment insurance or health insurance benefits during my period of unavailability. Thank God I am not in this situation, but if I were I would do two things:

1) Be honest.

2) Find some other way to make my living as soon as possible.

MAKE FRIENDS WITH EACH HIGH SCHOOL'S OFFICE STAFF

The office staff are your back-up, when you are in the classroom. Yes, I mean like a cop has back-up. Whenever he is about to go into a dangerous situation, a cop calls in for back-up. The people he calls make sure his back is covered and no one can sneak up on him from behind, so to speak. Back-up is your safety net, your life line. It's who you call when you see trouble coming, and hope someone can get you out of trouble. Back-up is a big deal. All that I know about cops having back-up is from fiction, but it is instructional fiction, so I am going to stretch the analogy.

I hate movies where there are bad cops who don't back up the good cop. The good cop is all alone out there, hiding behind a car with the last bullet in his gun. The bad guys are about to close in. The good cop has called in for back-up, but it hasn't shown up. My husband loves these movies, so I have seen lots of them, but I hate them. I hate these movies because this is my worst nightmare: being stranded in the classroom with no one to call to back me up.

However, I do love one aspect of these "bad cop" movies and TV shows. I love how the good cop's buddy always saves him. Make sure you have at least one buddy in each high school's office.

Realistically, one buddy is not enough. He or she might be absent or on another call when you need back-up. It is in your best interest to be friendly toward everyone on staff in the office of each high school where you substitute teach. If this is obvious to you, great! You are adept at the social graces and should live a long and prosperous life. I might know a thing or two that hasn't occurred to you, though, so please read on, Grasshopper.

Making friends in the workplace is as simple as following the golden rule: Treat other people the way you would want to be treated.

First, imagine yourself in the other person's situation. Put yourself in their shoes. Picture yourself doing their job and having their responsibilities. It should only take a second. Next, from that person's perspective, consider how you would like someone in your current situation to behave. And then behave that way.

So, can you imagine what it is like to work in the office at a high school?

Perhaps I have the advantage here. I worked my way through college. Among various and sundry other jobs (pizza delivery girl, actress, singer, seller of men's suits, insurance policy analyst, collections agent, coffee bean salesperson, waitress, proofreader, telephone book deliverer, insurance claims adjuster...), I have been a secretary, receptionist, and clerk.

I bet the hardest part about working the front desk in the

school office is keeping up with all the phone calls from parents. One wants Junior's homework sent home because he is out with the measles. Another wants to know why softball practice was canceled. The next caller wants to speak with a math teacher who is busy teaching a class right now. I bet the office lady spends most of her time taking messages and sending them to other adults in the building with students who work in the office as "Teacher's Aids" (TAs).

If you were busy on the phone taking a message, how would you want someone who approached your desk to behave? I would want them to smile at me and then patiently and quietly wait until I was done writing the message for that phone call. That is exactly what I do whenever I approach the office lady's counter. I smile at her, and then I wait until she is ready to give me her attention before I say anything.

I don't bother the office lady on the phone from a classroom unless it is strictly necessary.

I don't call the office lady unless either:

1) I need back-up, or

2) Something is preventing me from doing my job.

If I do call the office from a classroom, I quickly identify myself, and then get right to the point. Here's an example of how I would call for back-up:

"Hello, this is Cherise Kelley in room A-131. I have a student here who doesn't think he needs to cooperate with my instructions."

Here is an example of how I might call if something less serious, but still important and not trivial, was preventing me from doing my job:

"Hello, this is Cherise Kelley in room A-131. The light bulb on the projector just burned out. Can you connect me to someone who can help?"

There are many instances later in this book where I tell you to call the office.

Please use these examples to instruct you when you do call the office. The office lady probably is already on a call when you phone her, and she might have three more callers waiting on hold. Identify yourself and then quickly let her know if you need back-up, or if something is preventing you from doing your job. For anything that can wait, just go see her during your lunch or during the regular teacher's preparation period.

As soon as you get hired by a school district as a substitute, visit each high school's office and introduce yourself to the staff there, as a new substitute teacher.

Wait until after 9 for this visit so that you miss the morning rush and the staff are not too busy to meet you. The purpose of this visit is threefold:

1) Start making friends with each high school's office staff.

2) Check on where to park when you substitute here, and on all the items normally found in a substitute

teacher's folder, which are detailed in the chapter on the substitute teacher's folder.

3) Find out how early they open the office and can give you keys and send you to your assigned room when you substitute at their school. Some high schools have zero hour and can let you in as much as an hour before school starts. Others barely open 20 minutes before school starts. Some give you keys, while others send someone to let you in. All of this is good to know before you have an assignment here.

Because of lock-down emergency procedures that should also be explained to you at each school where you substitute, I don't personally choose to substitute in schools that won't give me keys to the classroom. A lock-down emergency is when a threatening person arrives on campus and the office sounds an alarm. Everyone goes into the nearest classroom, and the teacher locks the door so that the threatening person cannot get in.

If I don't have keys to the classroom, then I can't lock the door during lock-downs. No thanks. No amount of pay is worth being a sitting duck when a threatening person is on campus.

If a school tells you:

"No, we don't give keys to substitutes,"

then it is worth a try to ask the staff:

"Don't you think that is unsafe? What if there is a lock-down emergency?"

If you find out that a school doesn't let substitutes into the classrooms early, find out if you will be able to review the lesson plans before school starts. Ask if the lesson plans are at least left in the office where you can go over them while you wait for your keys to the classroom.

Regarding parking:

City schools might have very specific places substitutes are to park. Often, high-school teachers have assigned parking spaces, and sometimes students even do. Parking can be a touchy issue, so ask where you should park.

Besides her role as your back-up, the office lady might get you substitute assignments.

Many teachers ask the office lady to go into the computer and get their substitutes for them. Teachers have to tell her they are going to be out anyway. She is sitting at the computer anyway. It just makes sense for this to happen. This practice is also a carryover from the days before schools were computerized.

I have not personally had this happen for me, but I have heard from substitutes who were friends with office ladies who always got the substitutes the best assignments.

It's not what you know; it's who you know.

ARRIVING AT THE SCHOOL FOR AN ASSIGNMENT

Plan to arrive at the school the moment the office opens. Check your records for this school's bell schedule and this school's office opening time as soon as you receive a substitute-teaching assignment. If it is in your power to do so, and if the office is open early enough, get to the school 45 minutes before you are expected to start teaching.

I substitute for two high schools in the same district. Not only do the two schools have different bell schedules, but each school's schedule also changes daily.

Some days are block schedule days where only three classes meet for two hours each. Other days they have "late start" for teacher collaboration, "advisory" periods when students have the same class all four years they are at that school, or "student access" periods when students can get extra help from their teachers or make up tests.

I have subbed only at these two schools for two years, and I still don't have their wacky schedules memorized, because they are so variable. Keep a bell schedule at home, for each high school where you will substitute.

The bell schedules tell you what time each class starts, and by extension, when students arrive and you are on stage and expected to perform. Give yourself time to get ready for this by arriving early each morning. It's not always possible to arrive early. Sometimes, you get the assignment when school has already started, but when it is possible, preparation time makes your day go much better.

Park where the substitute coordinator or school office lady explained you should.

Make sure you roll up all your windows and lock your vehicle with your key so you can't lock your key in the car.

Walk toward the front of the school. The school office is almost always front and center. If you have trouble finding the school office, ask anyone.

Go into the school office and introduce yourself to the first employee you see:

"Hello, I am substituting for (regular teacher's name) today."

Either that employee will check you in, or they will direct you to the person who will.

The closer it gets to the time school starts, the busier the office will be, which is another good reason to arrive right when the school office opens. The next chapter is about what to get from the school office after you check in.

Bring to the school with you:

- Your lunch. See "The Teacher's Lounge" chapter.
- School district ID badge
- Lanyard for wearing keys around the neck in case of inadequate pockets
- Your user name, password, and instructions for taking attendance on the computer
- Copy of the school's bell schedule
- Cell phone
- Driver License
- Wear a watch.
- Pen and paper for writing a note to the regular teacher
- 5 or 6 sharpened pencils for students
- Business cards and a few paper clips for them
- Pencil in case attendance gets bubbled in on a form
- Dry-erase marker, in case those in the classroom are all dried up
- Headache relief
- Change for the occasional bake sale
- A handkerchief or tissues
- Sanitary napkins or tampons for yourself, if needed

Bring all this in something that is NOT a purse.

Do not entice the few dishonest students you might encounter to rummage through your purse. Do not bring into class anything that even looks like a purse. I use an insulated lunch bag. My purse stays at home.

Some school districts schedule substitutes with plenty of time to read the lesson plan and get the classroom ready.

Some school districts think ahead and get substitute teachers to school in plenty of time, but others schedule you right when students arrive. Typically, when teachers within the district request you for partial absences, they request you starting when students arrive. You need to arrive at the school in plenty of time to at least read the lesson plan, even if another teacher is in the classroom and you can't prepare the classroom.

Remember those bell schedules and school-office opening times I told you to get for each high school, from the substitute coordinator or from the office staff? This is why you need them at home.

SUBSTITUTE TEACHER'S FOLDER

Almost every school I ever substituted in over the last 20+ years provided me with a substitute teacher's folder for the day. Both high schools where I currently substitute provide these folders. They are kept in the office and handed out to the substitutes as we check in for the day. We substitutes turn the folders in with our keys at the end of the day.

In this chapter, I itemize what is in a substitute teacher's folder, and I explain each item in some detail. If you substitute at a school that does not provide substitute teacher folders, then get as much of this as you can from the school office – and make your own folder to bring the next time you substitute here. If I ever subbed at another school that didn't provide substitute folders, I might even volunteer to come in on a day off and assemble these folders for them.

The list of what is in the folders is on the next page. I go into details about all the items on this list a little later on in this chapter. If you are handed a substitute-teacher's folder when you check in at the high-school office, look inside for:

- School Office contact method for back-up
- This teacher's classroom numbers, schedule, and keys
- Emergency evacuation map for each classroom this teacher uses
- Emergency Procedures Bulletin (fire alarms and other alarms)
- Where in the classroom is this teacher's emergency backpack?
- Staff restroom key and staff lunch room key
- School Map, complete with staff restrooms and lunch rooms
- Today's School Bell Schedule
- Three blank discipline referral forms
- Hall pass forms, if required
- This teacher's scheduled lunch time (in schools that have multiple lunch periods)
- Instructions for reporting attendance to the office
- Student Handbook of school rules and consequences

Make sure you understand how to contact the school office before you leave it.

Some schools have fully functional phones in the classrooms, but others just have an intercom system. Make sure you understand how to contact the office using whatever means is available. Do not be embarrassed to ask how to operate the intercom. Many of these were installed in the 1960s and are quaint, to say the least. If you are to call an extension on the classroom phone to reach the office, then make sure the extension is written down someplace you can easily find it.

Some substitutes (and some regular teachers I know who work in tough schools) program the office phone number into their cell phones and keep their cell phones on them, for emergencies.

One of the schools where I currently work has the school office extension on a sticker on the inside of each substitute folder. The other school just has a list of extensions, and I always have to search through these extensions to find the number I need. When I am on the ball, I make sure and have the office extension written down on a separate slip of paper in my bag that I can grab when I need it. One of these days I will program it into my phone. Do this if you are the type of person who always has your phone on you.

If the office balks at giving you classroom keys

If they tell you they don't give keys to substitutes and the custodian or someone will let you in, remind them you need to be able to lock the classroom if there is a lock-down situation. A lock-down is where a crazed person comes on campus and the office sounds an alarm that means everyone is to go into the nearest classroom and lock the door. The sound of this alarm should be in the school's emergency procedures bulletin, which is on the above list of things for you to get for each school you substitute in, if they aren't in your substitute folder.

Emergency Procedures Bulletin

Get this school's emergency procedures bulletin and read it before you leave the office. If they tell you:

"Oh, there aren't any drills scheduled for today."

(Honestly, I have been told this!)

Remind them there could be an actual emergency. You need to know the sound of each individual alarm and what it means. There are a few: lock-down we just discussed, fire you probably remember, but there are others. Familiarize yourself with these procedures. There is a whole chapter on this later, but get these procedures while you are in the office.

Emergency Backpack Location in the Classroom

All the schools where I have taught since 2005 have had emergency backpacks. Each teacher keeps her own in her classroom, and it should be accessible to anyone, and not locked in a cabinet. The pack contains a first aid kit, water, and current lists of students enrolled in each class. The teacher is meant to grab this pack whenever an alarm rings. The Band aids and current class enrollment lists have come in handy at times, but be sure and tell the teacher if you used any supplies, in your note to the regular teacher.

See that chapter for more information.

Ask the office if the school uses emergency backpacks. If the school does, then the teacher should leave the location of her emergency backpack in her substitute folder in the office, or in her lesson plan, if the office doesn't have substitute folders. If she doesn't indicate where it is, then ask the neighboring teachers.

Staff Restroom and Lunchroom Keys

Teachers have to use the restroom during passing period, preparation period, or lunch. We are required to be in the classroom during class time. We have to dash to the restroom and back. I have written a whole essay on this in the chapter on when you need the restroom.

At most schools, the staff restrooms are locked, except for the ones in the teacher's lounge. Every teacher has a restroom key, and substitutes should get to use a restroom key, too.

Some teacher's lounges (lunchrooms) are also locked, so ask about this while you are in the office.

School Map, complete with staff restrooms and lunch rooms

Ideally, teachers should know their way around campus. Practically, as a daily substitute you don't have the brain capacity to memorize the floor plans and layouts of all the different schools where you work.

I only work in two high schools. They have identical floor plans, except they are oriented in different directions. I have been working at these two schools for two years, and I still get confused. Get a map. If the map doesn't indicate where the nearest staff restroom to your classroom is, then ask. Likewise ask if it doesn't show you where the teachers eat lunch. You can read more on this in the chapter on The Teacher's Lounge.

This teacher's scheduled lunch time (in schools that have multiple lunch periods)

Find out which lunch you have, before you leave the office. In schools that have multiple lunch periods, your dismissal time for one of your classes might be different, depending on which lunch you have. If the students try to get you to dismiss them for the first lunch period, you need to be able to confidently tell them:

"Nice try, but I know we have third lunch."

Today's School Bell Schedule

This is the start time and dismissal time for each class period. Ideally, teachers have the bell schedule memorized.

Again, substitutes go to many different schools. It is impractical to expect substitutes to memorize multiple bell schedules, but school staff often overlook this. Ask for a bell schedule. I only substitute in two high schools, but both have variable block schedules. This means the schedule varies with the day of the week. After two years, I still need to consult the bell schedule every day.

Each school also has special schedules for assemblies, minimum days, pep rallies, and a whole bunch of other variables. Get today's bell schedule.

Three blank discipline referral forms

These are needed to document why a student was sent to the office for discipline. Use them if a student is not cooperating with your reasonable and appropriate requests, or if the student vandalizes, is violent, or is grossly inappropriate (sexual harassment, for example). I tell you more about this in the chapters on the actual teaching and keeping students from wrecking the room and other horrors.

Read the items next to the check boxes on the referral form for guidance as to what needs to be written up. It is most practical to call the office and tell them the student is coming, in case he gets lost on his way down there. Some schools will send a security guard to the classroom to escort the student to the office. Most office ladies will send a runner to the classroom to pick up your referral form, once you finish writing it.

Hall Pass Forms

Log students who leave the classroom out on a sheet of paper that you keep by the phone in case the office calls for them. I explain this better in the chapter on preparing the classroom.

Some schools require official printed hall-pass forms for any student who is out in the halls. Ask if this school requires these, and if so, ask for a few. I have only taught in one school recently that required these, but in schools that do, you need to have a few. I make the student who needs to leave the room fill one of these out, and I only sign it once it is complete, in pen.

Most schools use permanent hall passes these days.

These are generic cards with the teacher's name and room number on them, usually on a lanyard that the student can hang around the neck and wear like a badge. These generally hang on the classroom wall next to the door, but sometimes they live on the teacher's desk.

In schools that use neither system, I have the student write a pass out on a small slip of paper which I only sign once it is complete with these items, in pen:

- Student's name
- Today's date
- Classroom number
- Student's destination
- Current time

Instructions for Reporting Attendance to the Office

I hear many substitutes speak mistakenly about attendance (roll) as if it is an afterthought. Wrong!

- Public schools get money from the state based on attendance.
- Schools think very seriously about attendance.
- If you do nothing else all day, take attendance!

Taking attendance (roll) is the one thing you really must get done each and every period that you have students.

In the district where I substitute now, I have my own sign-in for the computer system so that I can take attendance as a substitute, without having to sign in to the teacher's account. This is the most desirable system, but I have worked with other systems for substitutes to take attendance. I have bubbled the attendance in on sheets that got scanned in the office. I have phoned the office with the names of absent students. I have marked attendance in the teacher's roll book.

Before you leave the office, find out how you are expected to report the attendance to the office, and get what you need in order to be able to report attendance to the office.

Student Handbook including school rules and consequences

The best high schools have clear codes for student conduct which are printed out in booklets that go home with the students and return signed by parents. These booklets spell out the student dress code and the principal's expectations for classroom behavior and work habits, along with consequences for students who don't measure up to these standards.

Ask each school if they send such a thing home with students. If they do, get a copy of it and use it! If they don't, maybe your question will get their ball rolling.

THE LESSON PLAN

Whoever you check-in with in the office should tell you where the lesson plan is. Read the lesson plan as soon as you get it, to maximize your chances of getting your questions about your day answered before you have to teach the class.

Often, the regular teacher emails the lesson plan to the office. If this happens, then read the lesson plan right there in the office so that if any of it is unclear, you can ask the office secretary to call the teacher or email her back with your questions.

Sometimes, the lesson plan is in the teacher's mailbox in the main school office. In this case, don't empty the teacher's box. Just take the lesson plan. Teachers like to empty their school mailboxes themselves.

Most often, you will find the lesson plan on the teacher's desk in her classroom, or on the lectern or front table in the classroom. If she shares a classroom, then her plans might be on her desk in a teacher's office near one of her classrooms.

If the lesson plan is missing

If the lesson plan is missing, or if any of it is unclear, or if you feel you cannot follow the lesson plan for whatever reason, call the office lady and let her know. (You did make sure you knew how to contact the school office before you left it, right?)

The office lady might call the teacher for clarification, or she might send a student over with the emergency lesson plan for you to use instead, or she might send another teacher over to answer your questions. If you ask right away, there are many ways the office lady can help you with the lesson plan, but you need to ask as soon as possible.

What is the lesson plan?

The lesson plan is the regular teacher's instructions to you, the substitute, on how to run her classes while she is gone. Follow her lesson plan as closely as possible. Don't worry about getting everything on it done. Teachers often leave too much work, so that their students for sure will be busy for the entire class period.

The only time to worry is if you can't get the DVD to play or something else prevents you from having enough activity to keep the students busy for the whole class period. These are the types of things you need to know right away, so that the office lady has time to help you. There is a chapter in this book on time fillers that should also help you in these difficult situations.

Here is a typical substitute lesson plan:

Thank you for subbing my classes. I hope you have a great day. Mrs. Smith in room 311 next door can help you if you get stuck. Please leave the names of absent students and any students who give you trouble. I will deal with them when I get back. My seating charts are in each class section of the white binder on my desk.

Periods 1 2 5 World History – These are seniors, so they shouldn't be any trouble for you. They are working on class projects. The assignment sheet is attached. They can use the computers in the room. Some of them might need passes to take photos around campus. Only let one group go at a time. Remind them their second project progress papers are due on Tuesday.

Period 3 prep

Second Lunch

Periods 4 and 6 US History – These are freshmen, and they can get a little rambunctious. Have them read chapter 11 and write out the questions on page 287, along with their answers in complete sentences.

"Student Teacher will be in charge"

One really cool thing the lesson plan might say is that the regular teacher has a student teacher who will do all the teaching and be in charge. In this case, you just need to be in the classroom as the officially credentialed teacher. A student teacher is someone who is enrolled in a teacher-training program at a university and is doing an internship at the school. Student teachers get college credit for what they do, but they are not paid. Some of them are credentialed as substitutes, but you cannot count on this.

Stay in the classroom even if a student teacher takes charge there. If you are new to teaching, then just stay on the opposite side of the room from the student teacher at all times and help her monitor the students' behavior. When she walks to the right side of the room, you walk to the left side. If you have completed student teaching and have some regular teaching experience, then act as a mentor for the student teacher, unless his or her university mentor is there.

A few times a semester, the student teacher's university mentor comes and observes him or her in the classroom. If you get really lucky, you might be present when this happens.

Even if the student teacher or his university mentor tells you to leave the classroom, don't. You are a school-district employee. The mentor is not. He or she is employed by the university. You are being paid by the school district to be there. Only someone in the district office or the school office can give you permission to leave your classroom when students are present. Besides, the office lady might call you on the phone. Stay put. Just sit by the phone and observe, if it seems like the university mentor teacher thinks you will be in the way.

I enjoy acting as a mentor to student teachers when I substitute. I make it clear to them that I will stay back and let them handle things and they should just let me know how I can help them. Usually, they want to teach the lesson and have me just monitor student behavior. I get a kick out of answering their questions and helping student teachers.

PREPARING THE CLASSROOM

Once you have checked in at the main school office and found the lesson plan, go straight to your first classroom. Do as much of the stuff in this chapter as you have time for before your first class starts, in the order presented.

1) Find and read the lesson plan. Work out in your mind how you will execute each part of the lesson plan. Locate the materials and equipment you will need. Call the office if you can't find the lesson plan, don't understand the lesson plan, or don't feel able to execute the lesson plan.

2) Practice operating any equipment you will need (DVD player, computer-screen projector, document reader, Smart board, overhead projector...). If you need any help, go ask the teacher next door before class starts.

3) Write your last name and honorific on the board, near the computer where you will take attendance (roll call). I write, "Mrs. Kelley." Be careful to only use dry erase markers on a white board. Write today's date over or under your name.

4) Log in to the attendance computer and get the first class roll sheet up on the screen so you are ready to call roll as soon as the bell rings to signify the beginning of the first class.

5) Briefly outline the first class's instructions on the board. For the first class in the sample substitute lesson plan in the last chapter, I would write on the board:

-World History:

-Work on your project – on the classroom computers if needed.

-Second Project Progress Paper due Tuesday

-If your group needs to take photos, put your names on my sign-out list and write out a pass for your group with your names, today's date, and "Mr. Rain's World History, Room 309." I will sign it when it is your group's turn to go.

6) Prepare a sign-out sheet for students. Make columns for Student Name, Time Out, Destination, and Time Back. Whenever you allow a student to leave the room, have him or her fill out this sheet, of course leaving blank the Time Back column until he or she returns. This way, you will know where a student is, if the office calls for him or her. This is something you will leave for the regular teacher, too. If you explain that to students, it should cut down on requests to leave the room. Prepare this later if you don't have time before class starts (or, prepare some beforehand and bring them with you).

7) If there is still time before students start to arrive, then write the dismissal time for each class period on the board where you can see it from anywhere in the room. Even if you are not able to do this before students arrive, you will need to note to yourself what

time you eat lunch and when your preparation period is.

Stop everything and smile at students as they enter the room.

Teaching resembles sports in that you must be "on the ball" at every moment, or you will lose. What is different in teaching is that you have 20 to 50 students in the "court" that you must watch carefully at all times. Watch each student as carefully as you would watch a ball in play on a court.

Don't appear to be watching carefully, though. Part of the game of teaching is you must put on your game face and appear to be calm and confident at all times. With experience, you will be calm and confident at all times. For now, fake calmness and confidence.

Pay attention starting as soon as students start to enter the room. Make eye contact with each student and smile at him or her. Do not smile tentatively, but rather as if you know a secret that makes you very happy. Project confidence and calmness. Wave back if they wave. Say hello if they greet you.

Watch to see which students are particularly outgoing so that when you take roll you can be sure and learn their names.

THE FIRST FIVE MINUTES OF EACH CLASS

Start roll-call as soon as the bell rings to indicate passing period is over. Roll-call is a familiar, time-honored classroom ritual for two reasons:

1) Roll-call is a natural way to settle students down.

2) Roll-call helps you learn a few of the students' names.

In teacher-training college, they told us to take roll by the seating chart. This works well when you are the regular teacher, once you start to know the students' names.

I learned the hard way that for a substitute, taking roll by the seating chart is not a good idea.

Often, the regular teacher has changed students' seats without updating the seating chart. I have done this, myself, as a regular teacher. Here is the reason this happens so often:

Somehow, after dramatically telling Sally and Susie to switch seats on a permanent basis, going to update the seating chart makes the teacher look comical. Seating charts are one of those things that are a good idea in theory, but don't actually work very well in practice much of the time, especially not for substitutes.

A nice high-school principal clued me in on using roll-call to settle students down and learn some of their names. So, as soon as the bell rings, start the roll-call ritual by saying,

"I'm now calling roll. When I call your name, raise your hand and say, "Here."

Loudly call out each student's first and last name. Look up to see who answers, "Here."

Learn a few of the students' names by calling roll, if possible, and use these names a few times during the class. Learning students' names encourages students to cooperate with you and make this a great day.

Students should quiet down when you announce roll-call. If they don't, loudly and calmly say, "Please be quiet so that I can take roll." Continue calling the roll right away, as quickly as possible so students don't get the chance to get bored.

If a student does not answer, "Here!" when you call his name, call his name again. If he still does not answer, say:

"Absent, (student name),"

and mark the student absent. When you are done calling roll, tell the class who you marked absent so that students who did not hear their names have a chance to correct the situation.

If a student corrects your pronunciation of her name, say, "Thank you."

If the loud speaker comes on with announcements or the

pledge of allegiance, pause until it's over and then start right up with roll-call where you left off.

Briefly introduce yourself, right after roll call:

"Hello! My name is Mrs. Kelley, and I am your guest teacher today."

("Guest teacher" just sounds more pleasant than "substitute teacher." Use "substitute teacher" if you disagree.)

Take a minute to go over the instructions on the board with the class, so they know what they are expected to accomplish this class period:

"You are working on your class projects today, and your second project progress paper is due Tuesday. If your group needs to go take photos, please fill out this sheet here and then write your group a pass for me to sign when it's your turn to go."

If the class is doing a lesson together, rather than projects, then tell students to get out the required materials:

"OK! Everyone get out paper and pencil, and turn your math book to page 321!"

Walk all around the classroom next to the students. Encourage students to get on the right page, get their pen and paper out, or whatever they need to get ready. Do not start until most of them are ready.

If a student pretends she didn't know she was supposed to

be getting ready to start the lesson, smile at her as if you are in on the joke, until she starts getting ready for the lesson.

Another argument for roll-call

One time when I had a particularly mischievous student in class, I was able to call him by name right after roll and ask him to please sit down.

This rascally high-school freshman was so impressed with me for calling him by his name that he bragged on me for the rest of the period! Whenever someone would come into the room with a note, he would point at me.

"She learned my name faster than any teacher ever has!"

He was pretty good for me, too, and I know it was only because I bothered to learn his name. Look to learn the names of the less-compliant students. Roll-call is a time-honored ritual for just this purpose. It helps you learn some student names. Sometimes, just learning a student's name can work magic.

THE ACTUAL TEACHING

A lesson is anything you are leading. A lesson is also called "whole group activity," in teacher talk. Not every class you substitute will have a lesson. As we saw in our typical substitute plan, often students will be working independently – on projects or on a test. Sometimes, the lesson plan calls for you to lead a lesson.

While you are leading the whole class in any activity together, students are all supposed to be on the same page and paying attention – to you, to their book, to whoever is reading, or to whatever they are supposed to be writing or doing.

As I mentioned in the chapter on the first five minutes of class, don't start the lesson (or activity) without telling students what page to turn to and what materials to get out. Give them a few seconds to get ready. Don't start until most of the students are ready.

Keep your eyes out of the book and on the students.

During a lesson (or activity), keep your eyes out of the book and on the students, so they can't get away with passing notes or throwing things at each other or other antics. If they start to do any of this, stop them immediately.

First, try to non-verbally tell students that you are onto whatever they have planned, without interrupting the lesson. Hold out your hand for them to give you the paper airplane they are folding. Go get the trash can and hold it out for them to spit their gum. Use whatever gesture you can think of to communicate that they need to settle down and get back on task.

If non-verbal cues fail to stop misbehavior, then interrupt the lesson briefly to remind the whole class that you expect them to pay attention to the lesson right now. Say something like:

"Allison is reading, and we are all supposed to be reading along in our books,"

or

"Make sure you complete a page of notes on this film. Your notes are due at the end of class today."

If any students are still off task, assign one student to continue the lesson by calling on students to answer questions or whatever is needed. Then, go up and individually talk to the students who are still off-task. Use your judgment to assess why they are still off-task. Ask them, even:

"Why are you still not following along with us?"

Sometimes, the reason a student is not following along is simple: he needs a pencil.

I have gotten to the point where I bring 5 or 6 extra sharpened pencils to give to students so that they can be successful with the day's work. If you don't want to do this, then help the student borrow a pencil from a classmate. I'll tell you more on my philosophy about students coming to class unprepared in the next few pages.

Sometimes, a student is disruptive.

If a student is distracting her classmates instead of following the lesson, then privately, calmly, and soothingly remind her:

"If you aren't going to do the lesson, then there is no need for you to be here."

You are making a soft threat to send the student out of the room to the office. See what her reaction is. Often, this will be enough, and she will get busy, at least while you are looking.

If she continues to make it difficult for other students to concentrate, call the office lady and tell her you have a student who doesn't think anyone needs to be doing the work in class. The office lady might tell you to send the student on down, or she might ask you who it is. Chances are high that the office lady is familiar with this particular student and spends a lot of time with her. You can even put the student on the phone to talk to the office lady.

The point is: you have not let the student get away with

disruptive behavior. You have taken action.

That is what is important. It's up to the office lady to decide what the next step is.

If you are in a tough class where many of the students refuse to work, then you are not going to be able to send them all out.

In that case, your goal should be for those who won't do the lesson to allow those who want to participate to be able to participate. I would just appeal to them directly:

"Could you all please keep the noise down so that the rest of us can do the work?"

Say this calmly. Don't be gruff or indignant about it.

Getting upset, angry, or panicky will just entertain the students who are refusing to work. Trying to make them work will make them less likely to comply with your request to keep the noise down. Be nice and reasonable. Be low-key and dignified about it. Respect high-school students, and they are more likely to respect you.

Sometimes, a student doesn't even belong in your classroom!

Particularly when the regular teacher has left a movie, a game, or some other amusing lesson plan, you might get students in your room who are not on your roll sheet. I used to worry about figuring out who these students were and getting them out of my room. As I mentioned before, I used to imagine I could catch these uninvited guest students by taking roll with the seating chart or making my own seating chart based on where students were sitting. This would take up a lot of time at the beginning of class.

I have come to believe it is more effective to make a mental note of which students seem like trouble, and then try and learn these students' names while I call roll. I can tell which students might be trouble by the way they act. Attention-getting behavior, posture, or clothing is a pretty good sign of possible trouble. If I notice I didn't call a particular student's name during roll, I look straight at him or her and say to the whole class:

"OK, now would be the time to leave, if you are supposed to be somewhere else."

Most of them will just give me a silly grin then and leave, somtimes saying goodbye to their friends first.

I also believe that engaging the students who do belong in the room in whatever activity they are supposed to be doing is more important than spending ten or more minutes fighting over the seating chart. As I mentioned in the chapter on the first five minutes of class, seating charts are not something you want to fuss over too much because often the regular teacher has changed students' seats without updating the seating chart.

If you have to write on the board during class...

If you have to write on the board during class, then do so with your back to the side of the room, rather than toward the students. Always keep the students within your view.

Do not turn your back on them, especially if they are freshmen before Christmas. Turning your back on freshmen is just begging them to throw things at each other, or even at you. Freshmen are the worst about this, at the high-school level. The older students are usually past this childish behavior, but not always. Do not turn your back on them.

Writing on the board while facing to the side is a little tricky at first. Get a white board at your home or use one in a friend's office and practice this. Better yet, get all board writing done before students start to arrive in class, if you can.

If the classrooms in your school district have document readers, computer screen projectors, smart boards, or even overhead projectors, then lean how to use these. They let students see what you are writing, without you having to turn away from students.

Some kids come to class unprepared.

At least once a week, even at the high-school level, I have a kid who has nothing to write with. Sometimes, the student is faking this just to have an excuse not to do any work. Most of the time, the student truly doesn't have anything. It got broken, lost, stolen, or ran out of lead or ink. Kids also often don't have paper.

The first year I subbed, I lectured these kids on coming to class prepared, just as I remembered my own teachers lecturing my classmates. I'm sure I looked really silly doing this, especially since I was so young. I am embarrassed for myself, actually, looking back on that.

Then, I went into a teacher-preparation program at a university. There, a lawyer told us that public education is legally supposed to be free. This lawyer told us that teachers have no legal right to require that students or their parents provide any materials, not even notebook paper, pens, or pencils. He further said that in fact, laws exist on the books that say each child is to be given by the school a new pencil every 6 weeks. This was in California, but I am pretty sure most states are similar in this. I'm not a lawyer, though. Check with one if you want legal advice.

From that time on, I started carrying extra sharpened pencils around with me, at first in a fanny pack (it was 1989), and now in my businesslike black insulated lunch bag.

Whenever a kid tells me he has nothing to write with, I just give him one of these pencils. I buy them at Walmart with my own money and sharpen them myself at home. I probably could get the school office to supply them, but I say, "Don't sweat the small stuff." I help kids borrow paper, if they don't have any. I help kids share textbooks if they need to.

You know what?

My new helpful approach has made me much more effective as a substitute than my former lecturing approach was.

The students have what they need to do the work, and no more excuse not to do it. The students I lectured had every excuse to be cranky and difficult, not to mention defiant.

It's the helpful approach for me now all the way, with this

and with most everything that comes up in the classroom. This really opened my eyes to how high-school students are not quite adults yet and that some do need my help.

You do have to be careful giving pencils out at the middle-school level and even with high-school freshmen. They like to play this game where they break pencils. If I catch them doing this I get really stern with them about making a mess and tell them to stop immediately. It causes a power struggle if you tell them not to waste pencils, which are their property to waste, usually, but they cannot argue that this doesn't make a mess.

Walk around the room, no matter what the lesson plan says.

Do not stay at the white board or even at the overhead projector or computer. Not ever. Conduct the lesson as you walk among the students in a random, unpredictable pattern. Walking among the students is the single most effective thing you can do to make sure they don't make trouble. If you need to come to the board or the overhead periodically, then of course do so, but do not stay there longer than it takes to quickly write something. If possible, get a student to write for you.

As you walk around the classroom, check to see what students are doing. If it appears that a student has forgotten what he is supposed to be doing, then remind him. Gesture to indicate he should be reading along or watching the video or listening to the student who is speaking. Maintain eye contact until he acknowledges your gesture and gets back on task.

Thomas J. Peters and Robert H. Vaterman advocate the practice of "Management by Wandering Around" in their book, *In Search of Excellence: Lessons from America's Best-Run Companies* (New York: HarperCollins Publishers, Inc., 2004). On page 289, they write:

"If you don't constantly monitor how people are operating, not only will they tend to wander off track but also they will begin to believe you weren't serious about the plan in the first place."

This is a very astute observation.

Peters and Vaterman go on to assure you they actually mean you need to get up out of your chair and visit employees in their work areas. In the next chapter, I explain why substitute teaching at the high-school level is more like managing employees than it is like being a parent or a babysitter. Substitute teaching at the elementary school level calls for parenting skills, but at the high-school level you need management skills.

As you walk around a high-school classroom, look to see if students are playing with their phones.

Despite antiquated school systems' attempts to ignore cell phones out of existence, 99% of high-school students carry phones on them. Most teens are capable of texting under their desks or inside their pockets without even looking at their phones.

During a lesson, they are all supposed to be paying attention to the group activity. Do not let them get away with playing with their phones during a lesson.

Phone use in class when there is not a lesson going on is a controversial topic:

- On the one hand, students can access things on their phones that school administrators would not approve of. The controls that the school board has in place on the school computers don't work on students' phones. On their phones, students can access pornography, gambling sites, and even Facebook, Heaven forbid!
- On the other hand, a phone is a computer capable of much good. Students can use their phones as calculators. They can look things up on the Internet with them, usually faster than they can on a school computer.

Each school has to decide the question of phone use in class that is not during a lesson for itself. I give you advice on this in the chapter on the teacher's lounge.

By high-school age, students know that playing with their phones during a lesson is disrespectful. I give the entire class one reminder:

"If I see your phone or any other toys out during a lesson, I am going to take them down to the office where you will have to pick them up after school (or whatever the school's student handbook says)."

If you see any phones during the lesson after that warning, then follow through and do what you said you were going to do. Take their phone and give it to the office for their parent to pick up, or do whatever the school's Student Handbook calls for.

If a student won't cooperate and surrender her phone to you, then tell her to go to the office. Call the office and explain what happened. Tell them to expect her there with her phone.

Have freshmen and sophomores read out loud.

If the lesson plan calls for freshmen or sophomore students to read anything, then lead the class in reading it out loud, together. Reading aloud makes sure everyone reads. It keeps everyone on task. It doesn't give anyone a chance to dawdle or get rowdy. It also assists the weaker readers without calling any more attention to them than anyone else.

If the class is reading a play, then ask for volunteers to read parts. Write the parts and their readers on the board. Assign a student to be the narrator, and have that student read the stage directions, which are in italics.

If the class is reading something other than a play, say:

"I will pick someone to read the first paragraph. They pick the next reader, and so on."

If no one raises their hand when you say you are going to pick the first reader, then gesture toward someone and say, "You go first."

Walk around the room as the students read. If you need to read along in order to understand what is going on, then read over students' shoulders as you walk around the room. Do not hold a copy of the book or keep your nose in any book.

Keep your eyes on the students and what they are doing. Leave the teacher's book on her desk. It is best if you just listen, rather than reading along. Put the responsibility of "knowing where we are" on the students. Let them help each other find the right spot if needed. Let them help each other pronounce unfamiliar words.

You just worry about the big picture: all the students are in their seats, looking at their books. None of them are playing with their phones or sticking gum under the desks or passing notes or dropping sunflower seed shells into the carpet or throwing papers, right? Good.

Present individual reading time to juniors and seniors as a privilege that you can take back.

Junior and senior students and advanced sophomore and freshman classes can be given individual silent reading time instead of reading out loud as a class, but still walk around the room and stop them if they are playing with their phones, making a mess, or otherwise not on task. Present individual reading time as a privilege that you can take back, by saying something like,

"OK, you guys can handle silent reading, right? If I let you read this silently on your own, I won't have to take it back and have us read out loud as a class, will I?"

They will assure you they can handle it. Most of the time, they can.

If one or two students get off-task, just individually handle them as described above about the disruptive student. Don't punish the whole class by taking back individual reading time unless more than two of the students aren't doing the individual reading.

Calmly and nicely address individuals who aren't reading. Remind them they don't need to be in the classroom if they aren't doing the assignment. If they still won't read, then send them to the office lady, and call to let her know they are coming.

Often, individual or small-group work follows a lesson.

This is when students practice what they studied in the lesson. In math, this means working problems. In most other academic classes, work time is when students write out the answers to the chapter questions, or write a paragraph summarizing the chapter, or fill in a worksheet, or do some other pencil-and-paper task.

In teacher talk, small-group work is called "cooperative learning." Ideally, the small groups are focused on the task at hand, and not talking about the game, the dance, the slopes, fishing, or anything else that is off-topic. In practice, groups are going to chit chat when there is a substitute teacher in the room.

The regular teacher has the power of the grade book to hold over students' heads if they talk off topic. A substitute can only leave a tattle note for the regular teacher, indicating that some of the students were chatty. You have no idea what the regular teacher is going to do about this, if anything. On the one hand, she might reduce students' participation points based on your report, but on the other hand, she might be one of those teachers who only gets annoyed by tattlers and makes sure she never requests you again.

I only tattle about things a teacher can check off on a referral form — cheating, vandalism, profanity that is directed at someone, violence...

I pick battles I can win.

As I walk around the room during small-group work, I remind students:

"It's OK if you are talking, too, so long as you are also getting your work done."

I pause and let each group show me how much work they have done. I praise adequate amounts of finished work, and I gently prompt groups who need to step up the pace a bit. I say something like:

"OK, more math, less talking!"

During individual work time, I let students listen to their iPods:

"So long as the rest of us can't hear it, and you tune me in whenever I make announcements."

The high schools where I substitute teach leave student iPod use up to each individual teacher's discretion, but policy on this varies greatly with each school district and even between schools in the same district. Get a feel for what is allowed in each school. There is more on how to do this in the chapter on the teacher's lounge.

Sometimes, the lesson plan calls for

students to take a test.

This is actually one of the easiest lesson plans for you, the substitute. If it is a short test, you can kill a few minutes at the beginning of class by giving students time to study their notes. Don't give them more than 5 minutes to do this, or they might lose focus and get bored and rowdy – especially freshmen.

Before handing out a test, say:

"OK, clear your desks of everything except (whatever they need in order to complete the test, usually a pen but sometimes a number 2 pencil, and a calculator, if the lesson plan says it is allowed on a math test)."

While students are clearing their desks, divide up the tests into piles, one for each row or cluster of desks so that you only have to hand 5 or 6 piles to 5 or 6 students and then the students can get the rest of them passed back or passed around.

Tell students where to put their tests when done, and remind them that after they turn in their tests they need to do something quiet at their desks until everyone is done. Just before you hand the 5 or 6 piles of tests to 5 or 6 students to start passing them back, say words to this effect:

"There is to be no talking during the test. If you have a question for me, then please raise your hand and I will come see you. I cannot help you with the answers, but I might be able to help you understand a question. Do not ask your neighbor. **If you are playing with your phone, talking, or whispering, then I will assume you are**

cheating and I will tell your teacher. Here are the tests. Take one and pass them back. You can start as soon as you get your test. No more talking."

Anti-cheating measures for tests

Walk around the room during a test, too. Students are capable of using their phones to cheat on tests by texting professional "answer" services such as ChaCha. If you don't believe me, **text any test question to 282282 and see how quickly you get an answer**.

If you catch a student fiddling with his or her phone during a test, confiscate the phone and do with it whatever the school's student handbook says. Let the student finish the test, but leave the regular teacher a note, explaining what happened.

If you see a student copying off another student's paper, or if they are telling each other the answers to the test, then calmly point to an empty desk and ask the copying student to move there. Without making a production of it, set that person's paper aside when he is finished, to give to the regular teacher with a note explaining what happened.

If you hear general talking during a test, tell the class:

"Even if you are done, please remain quiet until everyone is done. The people who are still working deserve to have it quiet."

If almost everyone is done and you hear talking, say:

"There are a few people still working on the test. Please remain quiet until I tell you everyone is done."

I usually tell students that after they turn in their test I don't mind if they play with their silenced phones or listen to their music through ear buds while they are waiting for everyone else to finish. However, make sure this is acceptable at this school before you allow it. Ask the regular teachers in the lunch room what they do.

If the lesson plan asks you to correct the tests

Is there an answer key?

If there is not, it is best to leave the tests alone and mention the lack of an answer key in your note to the regular teacher.

If you have an answer key and there is enough time after students finish taking the test, then pass out the papers so that no student gets his or her own paper, and then have the students correct the tests with your help. Say:

"Raise your hand if you have your own paper."

If any students raise their hands, tell them to trade around until no one has his or her own paper. Next, say:

"Write cb at the bottom of the paper you are correcting, and then write your name." (The cb stands for "corrected by.")

Next, go through the answer key and read off the answers, waiting while students mark the papers. When that is all done, say:

"OK, put the number they got right at the top of the paper, show it to the person, and then pass the papers forward."

This should get most of the papers corrected before school gets out. Leave the papers in neat stacks on the teacher's desk. Include in your note to her how you corrected the papers.

Do not limit your ability to wander around the classroom.

You need to be able to walk around the room so you can check on any student at any time.

Don't stand at the white board and keep score while the class plays a game. Ask for a student volunteer scorekeeper. Monitor the scorekeeper and replace her if she doesn't stay on the ball. Use your judgment if she doodles on the board or talks out of turn. If she's entertaining the other students in a good-natured way, I let it continue. It's just a game. However, if the scorekeeper's doodling or commentary is annoying the rest of the students, I stop it.

If you have to fiddle with the computer every few minutes to keep a movie playing, get up right after you move the mouse and make a circle around the room as you come back to move the mouse again.

If you are grading oral reports (I have been asked to do it more than once), then put the score sheet on a clipboard or on a thin, lightweight book, so you can take it with you as you walk around the room.

Again:

Walk around the room.

Encourage students to do what they are supposed to be doing. Supervise them.

TIME FILLERS

Every beginning teacher worries about keeping the students busy for the whole class period. People warn you that students who aren't busy get bored, and bored students make trouble.

This is very true. You do want to keep the students engaged in activity so they don't get bored.

Up until the advent of the Internet, most books on substitute teaching consisted largely of worksheets the substitute could photocopy and hand out to kids in the event the regular teacher hadn't left enough work to keep the students busy all period. This book doesn't have any worksheets in it, for two reasons.

1) All of the classrooms I substitute teach in today have computers hooked up to both the Internet and a projector. There are millions of free worksheets to choose from on the Internet that you can project for students, if that is what you want to do with any extra time. If you are not very Internet savvy, just go to a website called "Google." In Google's search box, type in "free worksheet" and whatever grade and subject you are subbing. If you don't know how to get the computer to project onto the screen, ask a neighboring teacher to help you – if you have your heart set on giving students extra work to fill any

extra time.

2) High-school students are pretty savvy to the educational process, though. They are likely to realize that any extra work you give them is busy work that won't count toward their grade. In other words: crossword puzzles, word searches, mazes, or coloring might keep kids busy in elementary school, but high-school students will very likely sneer at this busy work. They might even make fun of you for providing it, and then what will you do? I recommend you don't even insult high-school students' intelligence with time-filler worksheets.

Unfortunately, busy work is about the extent of what all the experts in the teacher-training field offer, for the purpose of keeping students engaged for the rest of the class period, after they finish the lesson. It is my impression that the vast majority of these textbooks are written with elementary students in mind, with just minor editorial comments for high-school substitute teachers. This is a sad disservice to high-school substitute teachers, who still face the question of what to do with those last five or ten minutes of class time.

The solution lies within the very nature of teenagers: they are social creatures.

If left to themselves, most teens will sit and talk. That can work to your advantage. With juniors and seniors, I often just tell them they can sit and talk after they finish their work. I do have a rule that they must stay seated. This cuts down on the chaos and keeps their behavior relatively tame. For more on how I enforce this rule, see the chapter on How To Keep Students from Wrecking the Room, and Other Horrors.

I even tell juniors and seniors they can go ahead and play with their phones after they finish their work. However, restrictions on this vary greatly from district to district and even from school to school. Make sure this is OK before you allow it. For ways to check if this is OK, see the chapter on The Teacher's Lounge.

Freshmen and sophomores will usually love it if you start them playing a game when they finish work. If the whole class is working together, then you can play a noisy game such as hangman, charades, "Guess What I'm Drawing," or even "Heads Up, Seven Up." A game keeps them all engaged. Engaged students don't get bored. Bored students make trouble.

Game Instructions

Students should all know these games already, but it will help you mediate any disagreements if you know the rules as well.

Hangman:

Choose one student to go to the white board with a dry erase marker. This student chooses a word or phrase that the other students have to guess, and marks out blank lines for all the letters in the word or phrase. Suggest they use vocabulary words, or terms relevant to what they are studying.

The other students raise their hands, and when called on provide one-letter guesses. The "up" student fills in the blanks with correctly guessed letters.

If a letter is guessed, but is not part of the word or phrase, the "up" student starts or adds to the stick figure of a man hanging at the gallows.

The "up" student wins the game if he or she manages to hang the stick man. A student who correctly guesses the word or phrase before this happens wins and gets to be the next "up."

Charades:

The "up" student acts out the words in the title of a movie or TV show. No props may be used and the student may not speak. The other students all shout out guesses until the student who correctly guesses the title is the next "up."

Guess What I'm Drawing:

The "up" student draws pictures depicting a movie or TV show. No letters or words may be used, and the student may not speak. The other students all shout out guesses until the student who correctly guesses the title is the next "up."

One-Word Story:

Get all the students into a circle. Explain that you all are going to make up a story together, but each person is only going to say one word at a time. Explain that the turn will go around the circle. At each person's turn, the one word they say has to be the right part of speech to continue what the last person said. The easiest way to start is if you say, "Once." Students can continue with "upon" "a" "time," or any variation that makes sense.

Heads Up, Seven Up:

The teacher picks seven students to be "up." The seven "up" students come stand in front of the class as they are picked.

The teacher says, "Heads down, thumbs up."

All the other students close their eyes, rest their heads on their folded arms, and put one thumb up. The seven "up" students each tap one different student's thumb, and then return to the front of the room. As a student's thumb is tapped, the student folds the thumb down, to show that it is taken.

When all the "up" students have returned to the front of the room, the teacher says,

"Heads up, seven up!"

The seven students whose thumbs were tapped stand up. The teacher calls on them one by one, to guess who tapped their thumb. If a student guesses correctly, then he or she goes up and the student who tapped his or her thumb sits down.

"Teacher":

Choose a student to be the "teacher" first. This student stands at the front of the room, facing the rest of the students. The rest of the students all stand at the back of the room, across the back wall. The student who is "teacher" turns to the board and writes a sentence as fast as they can, complete with a period, and then turns back toward the class.

While the teacher's back is turned, the other students try to quietly sneak up to the front of the room and touch the board. The first one to do so wins and gets to be the next teacher.

Students who make noise, you tell to go back to the back. Students who the "teacher" sees moving, he or she sends to the back to the back.

If games aren't your thing

If games aren't your thing and you don't feel comfortable letting students just socialize – while sitting in chairs – here are some other "sponge" activities you can use to soak up extra class time and keep high-school students engaged those last five to ten minutes until the bell rings:

Start a class discussion.

This is particularly successful at engaging students if some significant event is coming up, such as The Olympics, prom, income tax day, or Christmas – or if some big news just happened, such as the election of a new President. You can also base discussions on the lesson if they just read a story or a chapter in history or science.

I find that the best class discussions are less formal affairs that I start one-on-one with a student. Other students join in, and I let them discuss while I go across the room and start that same discussion or another discussion with some other students. I work the room, keeping the conversation lively.

Bring a G-rated movie to show the class if there is extra time.

A PG-rated movie is OK for high school if it relates to the lesson, usually. Most schools show freshmen Franco Zeffirelli's "Romeo & Juliet," for example.

However, you probably don't know what the lesson plan is before you leave the house. You are better off grabbing something G-rated. It also has to be a very entertaining movie just in and of the five or ten minutes students will see. Disney cartoon features of classic stories such as "The Hunchback of Notre Dame" often work well for this. They are entertaining, but you could argue they are also educational, if an administrator or parent happens to enter the classroom while you are showing it.

Remember, though, that each classroom has a different way to show movies, and it can be difficult to figure out how to show a movie in any given classroom, at short notice. The students often help me with this if I ask them.

Do a trick.

Say to the kid nearest you, "Hey, I have a trick I would like to show you all, but I need everyone to sit down and be quiet." You might have to give the kid a description of your trick, but you will usually be able to enlist his help in getting everyone settled and quiet.

If you do magic tricks, these work well.

I do ventriloquism. I say the alphabet and all the students' names through my nose, without opening my mouth or moving my lips. There is a video of me doing my ventriloquism on my Amazon author page. If it is not there, then search YouTube for "Real Ventriloquism by Cherise Kelley."

Other teachers have done math tricks, card tricks, and even "mind reading" tricks to keep students engaged those last few minutes, especially right before lunch. It's up to you to come up with something entertaining, but if tricks appeal to you, then I have no doubt you will!

HOW TO KEEP HIGH-SCHOOL STUDENTS FROM WRECKING THE CLASSROOM, AND OTHER HORRORS

When speaking with teachers and school administrators, whatever you do to keep students from wrecking the room and other horrors is called "classroom management," but I didn't expect you to know that when reading the table of contents. Most books for substitute teachers tell you to be very strict and firm with students, and to give them busy work to keep them under control. Most books for substitute teachers are written with elementary school students in mind.

Instead of trying to dominate high-school students, be someone with whom students want to cooperate. Most of them are still legally kids (and if you are over 40 they really look like kids), but in a few short years these students will hopefully be out on their own, fending for themselves. More than anything, high-school students want to be grown-ups. They will want to cooperate with you if you treat them like grown-ups, but not quite as your peers.

When substituting at the high-school level, be less like a parent and more like a boss.

In kindergarten through second grade, classroom management is all about intimidating students. Teachers construct "discipline systems" that boil down to intimidation. For young students, this works if it is done consistently.

In grades 3 through 8, teachers' discipline systems are more geared toward peer pressure and competition:

"Table 2 may go, and table 4. Table 1, you need to clean up those colored pencils..."

I am not knocking this; I am saying that once kids are in high school, this parental type of intimidation stops working, especially for daily substitute teachers.

When you are a daily substitute at the high-school level, what works is treating the students the way an employer would, rather than the way a parent would. Have a businesslike but friendly and helpful attitude. Be there to help the students with their work habits. Realize that this is their classroom, and you are a guest. Treat the students as you would want to be treated, if you were sitting in one of those student desks.

Raise your voice if needed, to be heard, but don't yell.

Don't talk down to high-school students.

Don't treat high-school students like children (well, except freshmen, until after Christmas).

Respect high-school students, and they will be more likely to respect you. That is my "high-school substitute classroom-management style" in a nutshell, but I am going to go on about it for a whole chapter to help you picture what it looks like, treating students like adults, but not quite as peers.

I like high school because the students are old enough to understand reason.

Most high-school students listen to reason. Not all of them do; there are exceptions. But, the vast majority of high-school students realize that:

- School is for their own good.
- They might as well take advantage of this education while it is being offered to them for free.

Keep this in mind in your dealings with high-school students. Remind them this is their education and they should be soaking up as much of it as they can in the time they are allotted to be in school, because sooner than they think they will be out on their own, trying to make a living.

One mistake I hear teachers make with this line of reasoning is telling students their grades are their pay for doing their schoolwork. Wrong. **Learning is their pay for doing the work in school.** Grades are a measurement of their learning, but grades are not the goal of their schoolwork; learning is. This is the major difference between school and a job: school is for the benefit of the worker.

Reminding high-school students that their work will

benefit them is a good motivator so long as the work is not busy work. If their regular teacher left them busy work, then allowing students to socialize while they work is a good motivator.

Approach high-school students from the role of a helper.

Help the students be successful in learning from their lesson and/or their work for the day. Make them glad you are there. Dazzle them with knowledge. Impress them with how much you know about the real world they will be entering after they graduate. Help them transition from childhood play to adulthood work ethics. As you walk around the room, say things like:

"Oh yeah, I remember studying that. What is the most interesting part of it to you?"

"Oh, hey, it's OK if you talk, too, but make sure and get your work done!"

"Wow! I really like the way that looks!"

"Good job with that!"

Remind students to get back to work, but do it in a low-key, one-on-one, non-threatening way. Inspire them, rather than trying to order them. Do order them if it comes down to safety or respecting you or each other, but order them politely and professionally.

You have no real authority, as a short-term high-school substitute teacher.

As a high-school substitute who is just in this class for a day or two, do not try and lay down the law like a regular teacher does on the first day of school (unless it is the first day of school, and then Heaven help you. I don't accept substitute assignments for the first week of school.) High-school students will resist if you come on too strong when you have no real authority. It's their natural teenage tendency. Unlike younger students, high-school students realize that:

- You don't grade their work.
- You probably aren't allowed to contact a student's parents.
- Your authority comes through what you tell the regular teacher, and what the regular teacher will do about that.

Some regular teachers have had the foresight to promise their classes a pizza party if they are good for the substitute, and to let me know about this promise in their lesson plans. Now, that gave me some real authority in that teacher's classes!

However, in most classes you don't know what the regular teacher will do about your report on how the class behaved. The students have a pretty good idea how much weight their regular teacher will give your report, but they are not a reliable source of this information. Don't count on your ability to threaten a high-school student with a bad report to the regular teacher.

Don't be too sure you can get rid of a student by referring him to the office, either. Sometimes you can, especially if you are friends with the office lady. However, other times the office sends him right back to you. Don't count on being able to hand out any kind of punishment at all, as a short-term high-school substitute teacher. Humbling, isn't it?

Go in with the humble attitude of a helper that students will want to cooperate with, and your day will go much better than if you go in thinking you are a lion that students fear. High-school students don't fear substitutes, but if you are a helpful substitute, they often are glad you are there.

Substitute-teaching in a high-school classroom is like managing a business.

Your management goals are for students to:

1) Complete the assignment, and

2) Leave the classroom in good shape.

The thing that is different from running a business is that the students are not only your "employees," but students are also your customers.

You want to retain your customers; they are what keeps any business afloat. It really helps to keep this in mind when you substitute teach. High-school students are much more aware that they are your customers than younger students are, and this factor does come into play with them, unlike with younger students.

Your approach to high-school students has to be one of "good customer service." Students will cooperate with you and even cheer you on if they feel you are adding value to their school day. Help them, but don't do the work for them. Don't give them the answers, but do help them find the answers. Do remind students who are off-task to get back to work, especially if they are disturbing others, but do this politely and professionally.

Call the office lady for back-up if any of the students refuses to comply with your reasonable and appropriate requests.

Then and only then do you become the parent-like teacher more commonly found in an elementary school classroom. I know this worry is at the back of your mind, making you want to take a hardline approach to subbing any class, even a high-school class, especially at first:

"What if the students won't listen to me?"

You call the office lady for back-up, that's what. This will work so long as you have not managed to make an enemy out of the office lady. See the chapter on making friends with the school office staff for more on how important this is.

Some teachers in a tough inner-city school district I worked for put the office lady's number on speed dial on their cell phones.

They silenced their cell phones and kept them on their persons at all times, ready to whip out and speed dial the office if needed. You could do this, too. It is probably a good idea, if nothing else for the security it would give you, knowing how close your lifeline is at all times.

But don't show the students how worried you are about this. If you are not calm and confident, then fake it until you are. Do get some real confidence by meeting goals that you set for yourself, but in the meantime, put on a confident and calm face. Take deep breaths whenever you get nervous or anxious. One real key to holding a classroom together is don't try to do too much, yourself.

Be a group facilitator and a resource.

Lead the lesson, but delegate reading, score-keeping, and anything else you can to students. Get students involved in doing as much of the work of keeping the lesson going as possible. Please see the chapter on the actual teaching for an explanation of what constitutes a lesson as opposed to work time, which has different rules for student behavior.

When it comes to reading out loud (which you always do for plays, and with freshmen, for anything), make high-school students take responsibility for "knowing where we are" in the reading.

Don't follow along in the reading, yourself. Don't tell them what words to look for in the passage. Wait and let them help each other find the spot. Let them tell each other how to pronounce words.

Keep your attention on the big picture:

Everyone should be seated and engaged in the lesson, not playing with their phones or goofing off. Walk around the room so that you can monitor everyone's engagement in the lesson. Quench distracting activity right away, but in a low-key manner that limits how much it distracts the rest of the students, if possible.

You can even make a game out of students knowing "where we are" in the reading, if you want:

You can make a rule that if whoever is called on doesn't know "where we are," they have to do a forfeit before being told where we are, and then they still have to read. If there are a bunch of papers on the floor, picking up 5 papers would be a perfect forfeit. If the desks need cleaning, then make the forfeit to clean five desks. Make the forfeit whatever needs to get done to make the room more orderly. Freshmen and even sophomores love games of forfeit.

During individual or group work time, walk around the room, listening to students' discussions.

Volunteer information that will help. Help them find the answers in their textbooks. Make students glad you are there. Chit chat a little, but don't let students get too far off course. Never allow students to discuss inappropriate topics such as sex, drugs, or fighting. By being businesslike and professional yourself, teach students how to be businesslike and professional.

A student asked me once, "Why do you say 'That's inappropriate?'"

I explained, "We teachers are trying to get you students ready for when you have to live on what you make at a job someday. We want you to know how to impress your boss so that you will keep your job and maybe even get promotions. Inappropriate topics are those that you don't discuss while at work or on a job."

"Oh!"

Be an authority figure only when pushed, but push back immediately (and only figuratively).

Act at the first sign of any unsafe behavior or disrespect, to you or to another student. I'm sure you can recognize unsafe behavior (roughhousing, pushing, hitting...). Disrespect can be name-calling, ridicule, taunting, spitting, gestures, making faces, talking back, talking over you or another student, refusing to clean up a mess the student made...

In general, disrespect directed at you means a student is not cooperating with your reasonable and appropriate requests. The vast majority of the students should want to cooperate with you if you are helpful and friendly, but a few of them enjoy making trouble. Here are some guidelines for dealing with urgent situations in the high-school classroom, as a substitute teacher:

- If disrespect is directed at you, call the office lady for back-up. Tell her your name and room number, what happened, and that you would like to send the offending student(s) down there to talk to someone. If you don't know the students' names, then put one of the other students on the phone to tell the office lady their names.
- If disrespect is directed at another student, request

that the offending student apologize. Say something like, "Whoa! That was wrong. You owe him an apology." If the apology is forthcoming and diffuses the situation, great. That is the outcome you want. If it does not work, then again, call the office lady for back-up. As I said, some students enjoy making trouble. The office lady will probably not be surprised to hear that one of these students is making trouble. It is best to call her for back-up as soon as you realize the student is not cooperating with you. Don't let the trouble escalate into a fight between students or anything else awful.

- If students start roughhousing or play pushing or hitting, say firmly and loudly, "That's enough." If they stop and look at you, calmly explain that what they are doing is not safe and then remind them what they are supposed to be doing. If they don't stop, then as you approach them keep loudly saying, "Stop!"

One of my students broke the other's finger once, just from playing around. They are not to roughhouse on your watch.

These two high-school seniors were best friends. They were just goofing around, sort of play fighting in imitation of how girls fight, slapping at each other. One slapped the other's finger just in the right way and the other was screaming suddenly. I told them both to go to the office. Later, the principal asked me what had happened and I explained they were just being silly and it got out of hand.

Ironically, the worst case of non-cooperation I ever had from a student

was not only while I was a regular teacher rather than a substitute, but also from one of my favorite students.

She put a pink bandana inside the overhead projector while my attention was diverted. Before too long, it caught on fire. Another student grabbed the spray bottle for cleaning the white board and gave it to me. I used that to put the fire out.

By then, the fire alarm had gone off. The whole school evacuated. There was an investigation, and the pink bandana was found. The principal showed it to me and asked if I knew who it belonged to. I told him this student's name.

What is encouraging is that she didn't hold this report to the principal against me or view me as a tattle tale. This was in a tough school where many of the students were talking about gangs. Later on, her boyfriend pulled a stunt so he could get kicked out and attend the much easier alternative school. Some of the students tried to blame me for his getting kicked out, but she defended me and said:

"No, she had nothing to do with it."

The point is this student wanted to cooperate with me because we respected each other. She was a good student and really smart and good at English. I respected her as a person and called on her in class, praising her good answers. She told me I was the only teacher who had ever acknowledged she was any good at anything academic. Within the limits of her need to create trouble, she did cooperate with me, especially where I really needed it in her standing up for me to other students.

Some disrespect is more subtle, but still you must act.

If a student is playing with her phone while another student is reading out loud or addressing the whole class, I give the entire class one loud reminder:

"John is speaking, and you are supposed to be listening. If I see your phone during this whole-class activity, I am going to take it to the office and you will have to have your parent pick it up."

(Or whatever the school's policy/procedure is on this. Ask the other teachers in the teacher's lounge at lunch, if this information isn't spelled out in the student handbook.)

Follow through and actually do this, if you see another phone during the whole-class activity. Send any student who refuses to surrender their phone to the office, and call the office lady to let her know the student is coming.

I tell students who are cheating on tests to move, and then I make sure and set aside their papers with a note to the regular teacher. I call students on non-directed profanity immediately by saying, "Language!" Be very clear about what it means to act in a businesslike manner. Tell students immediately if they act inappropriately. This is mostly what they need to learn from you as a high-school substitute teacher: how to behave in a businesslike manner.

Learn the name of any freshman who is not working.

A freshman student who isn't working gets bored, and a bored freshman starts trouble. Just the fact that you know his name will settle him down in most cases. Here's how this is done:

Go away from the student who is not working and quietly ask a student on the other side of the room,

"See that guy over there who's not working? What's his name?"

Call out the guy's name to see if he responds. If he doesn't at least look up when you call his name, give the student who gave you the wrong name a teasingly scornful look and wait for the real name.

Once the bored freshman responds to his name, make eye contact with him and then gesture from across the room that he should get back to writing or reading or whatever he is supposed to be doing. Look at him until he gets to it. As always, if he gets belligerent then call the office lady for back-up.

Older students are less likely than freshmen to make trouble or get bored. They deserve the natural consequences of not doing their classwork, and they are old enough to monitor their own work habits. They can miss the points or do poorly on the test or have to do the assignment as homework. Of course do get on them if they start making trouble or distracting other students.

Seating charts are good for knowing student

names — in theory.

I think it is some sort of law in most states that regular teachers have to make seating charts and give students assigned seats. In theory, this helps a substitute or an administrator know who is missing from the classroom at all times. It is a noble goal which we all should strive to attain. However, as a substitute teacher, in practice I find seating charts a waste of time.

For one thing, most high-school students are savvy enough to realize you don't know their names. The moment they realize they have a substitute, at least ten percent of high-school students decide not to sit according to the seating chart. These ten percent collude with each other to trade seats and answer, "here" for each other when you call roll. They don't do this inside the classroom where you can hear them, but in the lunch room, the hallways, and the quad. Word gets out after first period, about which teachers have substitutes that day.

There are ways you can combat this, and in elementary and middle school you should.

(Hint: Make your own seating chart while you call roll. Tell the students you are going to do this, and that you are going to leave it for their regular teacher.)

However, in my experience, making a big deal about the seating chart in high school classes makes a substitute teacher look foolish and insecure. In high school, as a substitute, if you win this sort of battle, it loses you the war.

The first few years I subbed, I used to announce that I was

taking roll by the seating chart.

This was recommended in one of my textbooks, in teacher-training college. It was meant to threaten students into sitting in their correct seats. Really, all it did was remind the other ninety percent of the students that I didn't know their names.

My first few years as a substitute were very challenging. Over the years, I have picked up all the advice in this book from my own teaching experience as well as from talking with veteran teachers and administrators. Listen to it and learn what has made my life much less stressful.

Another reason seating charts are a waste of time for a high school substitute is:

You want your eyes on the students at all times.

Don't have your eyes on anything but the students unless absolutely necessary. Instead of taking roll by the seating charts, it's much better to use the time-honored ritual of roll-call to learn a few student names. Make eye contact with each student as you call their name. Just the fact that you might know their names will keep ninety percent of high-school students from misbehaving.

Some school districts have students' photos in the attendance computer in such a way that teachers can organize students' pictures into a seating chart that substitutes can see on the computer or printed out in the teacher's book. These are awesomely useful for identifying students who were uncooperative and leaving notes about them for the regular teacher. However, this needs to be done after school or during preparation period.

As I said earlier, during class you need to have your eyes on the students as much as possible, not on the computer, not in a book, nor on the seating charts. This next section is another reason I pretty much ignore the regular teacher's seating charts.

I tell freshmen and sophomores to remain seated.

Freshmen tend to throw papers whenever too many of the students are out of their seats, especially the boys. Even if they are theoretically throwing wadded-up papers into the trash can, this gets chaotic and messy far too quickly. The classroom is not a basketball court.

Whenever I have a class of freshmen (and sometimes even sophomores) and we are not doing a whole-group activity, I announce to the whole class:

"I have one rule: sit down in a chair unless you have to sharpen your pencil or blow your nose or something. Pick any chair you want, but sit down in a chair, please."

Allowing students to pick any chair they want softens the blow and makes them more likely to comply with my request to stay seated. The ninety percent who would have complied with the seating chart are almost always thrilled with me for allowing them to go sit with their friends. The ten percent who sat with their friends despite the seating chart no longer feel so smug. With both groups, I win.

If a student starts to get rambunctious in the seat she

chose, I do have the option of telling her to move, and I do reserve this option. I simply point to an unoccupied seat across the room and tell her, "Please move over there." As always, if a student refuses to comply with my reasonable and appropriate request, then I call my friend the office lady for back-up.

Making students stay seated is the key to keeping them calm so that they don't wreck the classroom.

Ignoring the seating chart is a small price to pay in order to keep them seated. Depending on the general mood in the classroom, I have even allowed a student to sit in the teacher's chair, so long as he moves it away from the teacher's desk. I never allow students near the teacher's desk.

I periodically have to remind students to stay seated, as the requirement to remain seated is not the norm for high-school classes. I just stand up straight and say loudly, to the whole room:

"Please sit down."

I stay standing and focus exclusively on getting everyone to sit down, before going back to the person I was helping.

Do not sit down, yourself, for more than a few minutes at a time.

Walk around the room, encouraging students to do what they are supposed to be doing. I say this in several places in this book because it is the key to keeping students busy: Walk around the room, and do so in an unpredictable pattern.

Just the fact that you might be right next to any student at the next moment prevents a whole bunch of horrors you could get stuck dealing with or face never subbing for this teacher again, such as:

- Sunflower-seed shells stuck in the carpet
- Pen marks on the desks
- Gum stuck in the carpet

As you walk around the room in your unpredictable pattern, check for gum chewing and bring the trash can over for students to spit out gum. Also check for litter and ask students to pick it up, as described in the chapter on having students keep the room tidy.

As explained in the chapter on the actual teaching, do not allow yourself to get stuck doing one task or standing in one spot in the room. Delegate tasks such as score-keeping for games so that you are free to "manage by wandering around" the room in an unpredictable pattern.

Students also behave better if you care about them.

Chit chat with students a little as you walk around the room. This doesn't have to be deep conversation; just say things like:

"That color looks nice on you!"

"How's it going?"

Many teens have two working parents, and they long for an adult to listen to their stories. Don't let students get too personal or inappropriate (see the chapter on not being a bad example), but otherwise lend an ear. If a student starts to tell you something inappropriate, say something like:

"OK, I'm sorry, that is an inappropriate story for the classroom."

If it is something the student should get off his chest, offer him a pass to see his counselor.

One time, I got really sad because of a student's innocent question. Some students had asked me if I wanted to be a regular teacher. I was explaining that in Washington State, substitute teachers have to have the same qualifications as regular teachers, and I prefer being a substitute. One of the students innocently asked me:

"Why, so you don't have to learn our names?"

"No! I would love to be able to learn all your names in the short time I have you in class. No, I prefer being a substitute because regular teachers have to do a lot of homework. They have to grade your papers and plan lessons and photocopy worksheets and fill out progress reports. Substitutes get to just help you with your work."

"Oh! That's good you can be a substitute, then."

That was one of the saddest things I ever heard a teen say, when she assumed I didn't want to know her name. Ouch! I try really hard to learn as many student names as I can, but even just subbing in two high schools, that is 4,000 names I would have to learn, and 1,000 of them are new freshmen each year. Try as I might, I couldn't possibly remember all those names. Sad, but true. I really admire office staff who do know all the students' names.

Keep calm.

You will undoubtedly have pranks pulled on you, as a high-school substitute teacher. Kids will hide everything from the dry erase markers to the teacher's edition of the textbook to the classroom phone.

They will stick gum on the earpiece of the phone so you can't hear whoever is talking on the other end. You might be so flustered that you don't realize the gum is there and you just keep telling the caller you can't hear. Don't ask me how I know this!

Do not get angry.

Do not ever use sarcasm or ridicule.

These are kids you are dealing with. Do not stoop to their level. You lose your influence over them as an adult role-model as soon as you lose your composure. Always be the bigger person. I know it sounds trite, but it is true. It shows maturity when you can remain calm and neutral, even though inside you are upset.

Trying to get revenge when high-school students make you look foolish will probably backfire, because a short-term high-school substitute teacher has no real authority. It is best if you can laugh it off.

Yes, I mean just laugh at how funny the prank was, along with the rest of the class. That will make it go away the fastest. That also takes the most confidence in yourself. If you can't manage to laugh, the next best thing is to act as if whatever happened does not affect you very much. Yes, I mean act as if you don't care.

If you can manage to be amused or apathetic when students try to make you lose it, you will prevail and last out the day.

One day when I was subbing in a high-school drawing class, some boys decided to go drag-racing with a few office chairs in the corner of the classroom. Two guys sat in the chairs and two other guys pushed them across the room, in a race.

There wasn't anything nearby that they could break. None of the other kids were paying attention to them. The rest of the students were happily working on their drawings, oblivious to the little office-chair drag-race going on in the back of the room. This is key.

If students who were working had become distracted, I would have stopped the drag-races. My job as a substitute is primarily to see to it that students have what they need to do their assignment. This includes a classroom environment free of undue distractions. I would have calmly walked over to the students who were office-chair drag-racing and said:

"OK, that's enough. Please put those chairs back where you found them and go back to your desks."

But, in this case, I sensed these kids were goofing off to get attention, but no one was paying attention. Again, if the goofs were getting the attention they craved, I would have stepped in and stopped them. As it was, I chose not to call attention to them by going over there. I hoped they would grow bored trying to get attention, and stop goofing off.

Yes, I also need to keep them all safe, but the chair drag-races were not unsafe. The students were not in danger. Nothing was nearby that could have broken. It wasn't a pottery class! It was a drawing class, and they were in a big, wide-open area. They were just goofing off, trying to get attention. Those are some judgment calls I made. Assess each situation for safety and act accordingly.

Anyway, my sense that these kids were goofing off to get attention and that they were frustrated that no one was paying attention proved to be correct when a fifth student tried to get me riled up. He came over and said:

"You shouldn't let them get away with playing on the chairs like that."

Uh oh. That clinched it for me.

Never let a student tell you what you should or shouldn't do — especially if they try to get you riled up.

This is a trap. The students are trying to get you to put on a show for them. Don't fall for it. Be the adult.

Keep calm.

A sixth student understood exactly what was going through my head. He told the fifth student:

"No, she isn't letting them get away with anything. She doesn't care if they do that."

Yep. Exactly. And, do you know what? They stopped doing it as soon as they realized no one was paying any attention to them. In teacher talk, ignoring clowning behavior to get students to stop doing it is called "extinction." It won't always work. Extinction only works if your action or reaction is required for the students to get the attention they want.

If the idea of laughing at yourself or acting like pranks don't bother you is new to you, then you had better practice this with some friends or relatives. Explain to them that you are getting ready to be a substitute teacher and you need practice dealing with difficult situations. Ask them to play a prank on you so that you can practice laughing at the prank instead of getting angry.

If you cannot manage to laugh at yourself, then practice making it seem like you don't really care and changing the subject. Say something like, "Alright, very funny. Now, let's move on." If you cannot manage this without showing your anger or crying, then you won't likely be successful as a substitute teacher at the high-school level.

Only laugh at a harmless prank.

Of course, if anyone is physically hurt or even in danger, it is not appropriate to laugh. It also is not appropriate to laugh if the students are being malicious or cruel.

Do not laugh if they use profanity at anyone or insult anyone or are disrespectful to anyone.

Call the office and ask for help if any of that even starts to happen.

Don't ever lose your cool, or "lose it."

If you get mad, don't show it. Uncontrolled anger is a sign of weakness. It takes strength and self-control to keep calm. Do keep calm. Redirect your anger into an effort to take whatever action will help the most in the given situation.

Getting mad might entertain high-school students, so that they try to get you mad again, and again.

Instead of yelling, stomping your feet, or hitting something, take a deep breath and then take whatever action will help the most. Remember, you can delegate clean-up duties to high-school students. You can also send one of the students to get another adult.

Most of the time, continuing the lesson will help the most. Call on a student and ask him or her a question. Put a student on the spot and change the focus of the class back onto the lesson.

The American Psychological Association has posted a helpful article on managing your anger, redirecting your energy when something makes you mad, and calming yourself so that you don't act inappropriately: http://www.apa.org/topics/anger/control.aspx If you would rather not type all that out, then use your favorite search engine to find:

"Controlling Anger Before It Controls You," by the American Psychological Society (750 First Street NE, Washington, DC 20002-4242 Telephone: 800-374-2721; 202-336-5500. TDD/TTY: 202-336-6123).

Laughing at a harmless prank often helps the most. Once you start laughing, you will actually start enjoying yourself. You will also release the tension in the room and the students will relax a little, too. Laughing with the students is the quickest, easiest way to get everyone on the same page and acting like you are part of the group instead of an outsider. So long as the prank is harmless, you share this experience with the students instead of you being a victim of them.

Here is a good article that uses a scientific approach to explain laughing at harmless pranks people play on you: http://bodyodd.msnbc.msn.com/_news/2011/07/26/71 43331-can-you-laugh-at-yourself-scientists-put-humor-to-the-test?lite If you would rather not type all that out, then search MSNBCnews.com for: Body Odd: Rita Rubin: "Can you laugh at yourself? Scientists put humor to the test". As usual, the comments are almost better than the article.

Treat high-school students as if they were your treasured employees.

Encourage students. Praise good work. Be in charge of the lesson, but don't be overbearing. Have a sense of humor and laugh off minor goofiness. High-school students are almost adults, and they respond best if you treat them like adults, but not quite as peers. Be more like a work supervisor, less like a parent. Stay calm. Do not get angry. Do not lose your cool. Say "Please" and "Thank you."

Here are some real-life examples of what it looks like to treat high-school students

like adults, but not quite like peers:

Situation 1:

It is the last 10 minutes of a freshman English class. All the students are done with their work. A few students have started to get up and wander around the room. Before too many of them get up, I go to the focal point in the room and raise up my hand to get their attention. I announce:

"OK, for these last few minutes you can sit wherever you want and just talk, but I do need you to be seated, in a chair please."

I wait and watch until they all sit down. A minute later one kid gets up. I calmly walk over to him and remind him,

"Please have a seat until it's time to go."

When he sits down, I say:

"Thank you."

Situation 2:

Before a sophomore science class started watching a movie, I told them:

"During the movie, if you have to communicate with your neighbor, make it a quick whisper so the rest of us can hear the movie. In fact, if you need to move so that you can whisper with the people you might want to whisper with, do that now."

We are 10 minutes into the movie, and two girls are talking and giggling loudly enough that it is difficult for the rest of us to hear the movie. I calmly walk up behind them and whisper:

"I don't want to separate you two, but the rest of us can't hear the movie. Can you please quiet down?"

They agree to quiet down, but a few minutes later they are just as loud as before. I pause the movie, look at one of them and say:

"I'm sorry. I warned you. Please move over there."

I indicate an empty seat across the room. After she moves, I say, "Thank you," and I restart the movie.

I let the student save as much face as possible.

I don't yell or lecture. I calmly and succinctly explain the problem the student is causing, and request that the student execute a solution, which I suggest. I always am polite about this, so that the student's dignity is not affronted.

High-school students already know better.

You don't need to explain too much about why their behavior is inappropriate, like you do with elementary students. Lecturing high-school students about bad behavior only makes them roll their eyes at you and tune you out. Short and to the point is best.

I constantly have my eyes on the students so that I can see problems when they just begin to happen.

In teacher-talk, this is called "monitoring."

So long as you catch a problem when it just begins, you can keep calm and just quietly talk to the students involved, without the rest of the class knowing or becoming aware there is any problem.

Walking around the room helps you do this better than any other advice I could give you. Have I mentioned before that you should walk around the room and not just sit at the teacher's desk? They say you don't remember something until you have read or heard it three times, so I hope I have said, "Walk around the room" at least three times.

When to use one of those three blank discipline referral forms and send the kid to the office:

Sending a student out of the classroom to see a school administrator is a last resort. It is your ace in the hole — something you know you can do, but try your best not to have to resort to.

Save your referrals for when a student won't cooperate with you. In other words, only send a student to an administrator when the student stubbornly (or violently) refuses to comply with your reasonable and appropriate requests. Realize that the administrator might send the student right back to you. Sending a student out of the classroom might only be a temporary reprieve.

Calling you names is another way a student can be uncooperative.

The one referral I have written in my 10+ years of substituting was for a girl who didn't like my sign-out procedure for allowing students to leave the classroom. She was clearly suffering from drug withdrawals, and that is probably why she didn't like my procedure. She wanted to leave the room at the same time as her friend left.

I calmly explained that only one person could leave the room at a time.

"You bitch!" she exclaimed.

I calmly picked up the phone, called the office, and explained what had just happened.

"Send her on over," they said, "and send your referral with another student once you finish writing it."

On the referral, I did not repeat the word the student used. I just checked off the "profanity" box and explained, "This student objected to procedures for leaving the classroom by calling the teacher a name."

Discipline referral documents go into the student's permanent record. They will be read by parents, future teachers, and perhaps even courts of law someday. It is advisable to write referrals in professional language.

Resist the urge to complain on referrals. Explain the situation as objectively as you can, focusing on the moment the student became uncooperative (or violent). Include facts, and facts only, on a referral form. Save sharing your feelings for at home with your spouse. I suggest you do not share your feelings on Facebook or any online chat environment. Many times those words get out to the whole world or worse to the kids you are upset about, scared about, angry about, or what have you.

When students ask to use the restroom / get a drink / go to a locker / library / counselor / other teacher

One way high-school substitute teaching is more like being a parent than like being a boss is you are legally responsible for the students assigned to your classroom that period (unless they are 18 or older, which some of the seniors will be). If the office calls and requests to see a student who is supposed to be in your classroom, you need to be able to tell the office where that student is — or that you marked the student absent.

Therefore, before you give a student permission to leave the classroom, have the student write his or her name and destination on a sign-out sheet, along with the time. Keep this sign-out sheet near the classroom phone. Explain to students that you will be leaving this sign-out sheet for their regular teacher. This should cut down on excessive requests to leave the room.

Only let one student leave the room at a time.

Tell the next student:

"Put your name under John's name on the sign-out sheet. You can go when he gets back."

There are two reasons for this:

1) It helps you keep better track of the students. You are more likely to notice that John has not returned if Mary keeps asking you, "Can I just go? John isn't back yet." If John is gone more than 10 minutes, call the office and let them know this.

2) It also encourages students to hurry up and return so that the next student can go.

If the school requires a written hall pass, ask the student to write it out. Do not sign the pass until it is complete in pen with:

- the student's first and last name
- the classroom number
- the date
- their destination
- and the exact time.

Do not allow students to block your view of the classroom.

This is another reason to ask students to remain seated except for pencil sharpening, turning in or picking up papers, and nose blowing. When they stand up, it is difficult for you to see them all. If you can't see them, you don't know what they are doing.

The other day, a student got up and came to ask me a question during the few minutes I was sitting at the regular teacher's desk. He stood right in front of me while he spoke.

I said, "Please move over there," indicating a space by the wall.

He gave me a puzzled and slightly hurt look.

"I can't see," I said, gesturing at the rest of the students.

His eyes lit up with understanding. He smiled at me and moved over by the wall.

Most of the time, students are innocent of intending to block your view. Still, don't let them block it. Insist that they be seated or at least that they move out of the way.

Afternoon classes are different from morning classes.

High-school students are nocturnal, for the most part. They stay up until the wee hours of the morning, socializing on their phones.

I hear them talking about this, and besides, I remember this from my own high-school days. We didn't have cell phones back then, so we couldn't text. We didn't even have the Internet. We had to socialize on the house phone, in whispers.

My step-dad gave me a bulletin board for my 15th birthday, decorated with a girl who had a phone glued to her ear. Weekends with my real dad, phone calls to my friends were long-distance and limited to ten minutes a day - so I read science fiction all night instead.

Teenagers are naturally nocturnal.

High-school students are not quite awake until ten or eleven in the morning. The first few classes of the day are usually easy, for this reason. However, after lunch, they are wide awake. Freshmen can be really hyperactive in the afternoon, bouncing off the walls, even.

Just because the first few classes of the day were easy doesn't mean the rest of the classes will be easy. Remember, you are starting over with each new class. You have to set the businesslike tone all over again. You have to learn a new set of names. On the plus side, last period's difficult students are someone else's problem now.

In the afternoon, do the lesson before you take roll.

Take roll while the students are busy working on something, in the afternoon. Get the chapter read and get the students started on their assignment, and then take roll while they are working on independent practice, after the lesson.

If the school has a rule about roll needing to be taken the first ten minutes of class and you have a whole-class lesson to do before students will be working independently, then give afternoon students a starting task to do. A starting task can be as simple as taking out a sheet of paper and heading it a certain way and writing a few sentences about their prior knowledge of the topic of the lesson.

This is especially necessary if you have freshmen in the afternoon. Be up in the front of the room when the bell rings to start class. If there are students who have not sat down yet, say loudly but nicely:

"Please sit down."

Give students a few seconds to sit down, but if they are still dawdling, say it again. Once they are all seated, tell then your name and then go right into passing out the assignment or asking them to get out their textbooks and turn to page x. Start the lesson right away, and save roll for when after students are working individually or in their groups, for the after-lunch classes.

You might even want to stand by the classroom door in the afternoon and greet each student as he or she comes in.

Make eye contact, and say hello, at least. It might be even better if you introduce yourself and shake each student's hand, if you can manage to be sincere and do this in a businesslike manner. The idea is to set the tone that you are in charge, but you are approachable. An added bonus to introducing yourself is students might introduce themselves, and you might learn some names. Any chance to learn some names is a good thing.

In the teacher's lounge one of my first years as a regular teacher, I made what I thought was a snide remark about how freshmen should not have solid subjects after lunch. One of the two PE teachers happened to hear me, and she surprised me by agreeing with me. She even said it could be arranged so that all the freshmen had PE and shop or other electives 5th and 6th period.

It's not just you.

Students really are much more hyperactive in the afternoon. Be prepared for this, especially if the regular teacher has freshmen in the afternoon.

After lunch is the time to really stress the rule that everyone remain seated unless they have legitimate business getting up (sharpening their pencils, turning in papers, or getting a tissue to blow their noses). Monitor the room carefully and remind students right away to please sit down. If a student starts to hang out standing by another student's desk, indicate a nearby chair and say:

"Please have a seat."

I even bring a chair over, if no empty chairs are nearby. Insisting that they all stay seated is second only to walking around the room, so far as strategies for keeping a lid on the chaos.

Interruptions

Speaking of chaos, are you familiar with Murphy's Law?

"If something can go wrong, then it will."

I posit a corollary which says:

"As soon as you get all the students quiet and you are ready to explain something, the classroom telephone will ring."

When I answer the classroom phone, I say,

"(Teacher's name)'s room, substitute speaking."

You have to answer the classroom phone. It's probably your friend, the office lady, wanting you to send a student down to check out of school or see the counselor or something.

This is the main reason I have students sign out when they leave the room. I know who is gone and where they are. I just call out the student's name. If the student answers, I explain out loud that the office wants them and they should take their stuff. If the student doesn't answer, I look at my list and tell the caller where the student is.

HAVE THE STUDENTS KEEP THE CLASSROOM TIDY

A messy classroom makes students more likely to misbehave. Students who come into a messy room — candy wrappers on the floor, papers scattered everywhere, desks not lined up straight in their rows — assume the previous class got away with littering and being rowdy, so they figure they will get away with these activities, too. This is pretty accurate figuring. Remind each class to clean up after themselves, so that your next class doesn't enter a messy room and get the idea they can misbehave.

State Education budgets aren't what they were.

In the 1960s and 1970s when I was in school, custodians swept, mopped, cleaned and dusted every classroom every evening. Today's teacher is lucky if her room gets swept once a week, and mopped once a month. School custodians no longer clean or dust, in some of the school districts where I have taught. There aren't enough of them to do this anymore. There isn't enough money in the budget to hire them.

The regular classroom teacher is responsible for the cleanliness of her classroom.

I know this because I myself have been written up for having a classroom that wasn't clean enough, when I was a regular teacher and not a substitute. Students in "Teacher's Aid" (TA) roles often are assigned routine cleaning and dusting duties. I myself spent more than one evening scrubbing grime off students' desks, when I was a first-year regular classroom teacher who didn't have any TAs.

The tidier you leave her room at the end of the day, the happier the regular teacher will be with you and the more likely she will be to request you, next time she is absent. Your best guide on how to leave everything in the regular teacher's room is:

What kind of room would you want to come back to after you had been absent?

Leave the room neater than how you found it. This is easiest if you have the students clean up after themselves, every period.

Students eating in class

I hear the custodians complaining about rats in classrooms all the time. I hope that makes you shudder! Food crumbs also attract ants, mice, and other creepy crawlies. Schools make rules about eating in classrooms because crumbs cost the school district lots of money in exterminator costs. Each school has its own policy on this, sometimes leaving it up to the teacher.

It is difficult to enforce your own "no eating" rule if the regular teacher allows students to eat in class, but you can and must enforce a "clean up your mess" rule.

Unless the regular teacher's food rules are posted in the classroom or noted in her lesson plan, it is difficult for a substitute to know what they are, in a school that leaves this up to the teacher.

I give students the benefit of the doubt on this. If there aren't any food rules in the classroom and the students come in with food they just bought at the vending machines or on the other lunch period, I let them eat it. Kids are growing. They need to eat. I do remind them:

"All that is going to end up in the trash when you are done, right?"

It's amazing how effective reminders like that are. After a reminder like that, the student almost always tells me, "Of course!" and cleans up his mess. If I don't give a reminder, half the time I end up cleaning up after the student.

If the regular teacher does have "no food in class" rules in the lesson plan or posted in the classroom, or if the school has these rules and does not leave them up to the teacher, then I do enforce "no food in class" rules.

This means I don't eat in the classroom, either. In fact, I rarely eat in a classroom. I find it refreshing to head over to the teacher's lounge for lunch, and share some time with fellow adults. Besides, the custodians are my friends, and I don't want to make extra work for them, cleaning up crumbs or the vermin that crumbs attract.

Constantly monitor the room for cleanliness.

As you walk around the room during each class, take notice of any students who are eating. Remind them to put everything in the trash when they are done. Look for litter. Ask a student near the litter to pick it up. Ask nicely:

"Would you please pick up that candy wrapper and put it in the trash?"

If the student gives you a pained expression, say:

"I'm not saying it's yours, but we need to pick it up. Please pick it up and put it in the trash."

So long as you remember to have students keep the room tidy from the very beginning of the day, you should be able to stay on top of it. If you slack off on this, you should spend the regular teacher's preparation period in the room picking up trash. Turn the lights off and close the door so it is less likely anyone walking by will notice you doing this.

If you see a student littering or drawing on a desk

If you see a student littering or drawing on a desk, then enlist his help cleaning the room, after you remind him in a businesslike way that littering and vandalism are unacceptable. You can simply say:

"That is unacceptable. Please put that in the trash."

If there is any other trash around or anything else that needs cleaning or straightening, have the student you caught littering clean it up. This often takes the form of the student washing the desks. It could also mean he sweeps the floor, if there is a broom in the room. Find something for him to do as penance for littering or drawing on the desk.

Also leave the name of the litterer or vandal in your note to the regular teacher, with an explanation of what he did and the consequence you gave him (cleaning the desks, sweeping, dusting, picking up papers, or all of the above). You can find out his name by asking a student across the room. Look at the kid who you have washing the desks and say:

"What's his name?"

Call out the name the other student gives you, to check and make sure he responds. If he doesn't respond, look at the student who gave you the wrong name until he gives you the right name. Another way to get the right name is to check the student photos, if they are in the attendance computer. Do this during preparation period or after school, though. Keep your eyes on the students during class time.

Right before you dismiss each class

Tell students to put their desks and chairs back where they belong. Just make a general announcement:

"OK, it's almost time to go. Please put your desks and chairs back where they belong."

Wait to say this until there is less than a minute left until the bell rings, because their natural tendency will be to bunch up at the door after they do this. If there is more than a minute left, it is best to get them to sit down again. See the chapter on time fillers, for what to do in that situation.

Usually, the last class of the day puts chairs up on top of the desks so that the custodians can theoretically sweep the room. I say theoretically because in reality they only sweep once a week or so, but you never know if today might be the day they sweep. Ask a student in the last class of the day if they usually put chairs up. If they do, then remind the class to put the chairs up just before their dismissal bell rings, after they straighten their desks.

LEAVE A NOTE FOR THE REGULAR TEACHER

Leaving a note for the regular teacher is kind of like telling the person you came to the movies with what happened while they went to the snack bar. This note's purpose is to smooth the transition from you being there, to the regular teacher being in the classroom again. The regular teacher needs to know the big picture: what the class learned, what they didn't understand, and what the students need or expect to happen next.

Start a note to the regular teacher at the beginning of the day. At the top, write the date and "Substitute: (Your name)." Write each class period on the note. For each class, write in what applies from each of the sections in this chapter.

Be honest in your note. Tell the regular teacher how the students behaved for you and the amount of work that got done, but tell it in an objective, factual manner. What you should not do in your note to the regular teacher is complain. I have seen many of these notes that were left by the substitute who was there before me, complaining about everything from the teacher's room layout to the students' behavior. No one is going to request you to substitute for them again if you complain. One time, an administrator even told me she was throwing out the whiny note left by the substitute who had been in that classroom the previous day.

"She wrote a lot about what the students did wrong, but not much of any use."

In other words, the substitute complained and whined about student behavior through the entire note. She didn't leave any useful information about what work was accomplished, what page students read to, what questions students had, or any of the other things the teacher needed to know about how the day went.

Do take names.

Don't get me wrong; you do need to note some student behaviors. Write the names of students who are absent or tardy, and indicate which they were. Write the names of any troublemakers, along with a brief explanation of what the student did, and what consequence you gave the student. Here are some possible examples:

"I set aside (students names) tests because (student name) was copying off (student name)'s test paper,"

"I had (student name) clean desks because I saw him writing on a desk,"

"I asked (student name) to apologize for using profanity that was not directed at anyone."

For ideas on how to get these names, see the chapter on How to Keep Students from Wrecking the Classroom. To know what I consider trouble worth tattling on, see the chapter on The Actual Teaching.

Note any part of the lesson plan you didn't do, and anything extra you did.

One time, a geometry class lesson plan called for me to actually teach the class new material. I am credentialed in math, but each geometry book uses slightly different theorems. I would have needed to read the entire book up to the lesson in question. There was no way I could follow that lesson plan.

Instead, I used a demonstration on similar triangles that I found in the textbook, a few pages before the assigned lesson. Students had to cut out three similar triangles and staple them together in a way that showed the triangles were similar. I graded this assignment, since I had given it. In my note to the regular teacher, I explained why I had used a replacement assignment and what criteria I used to grade it.

Note unusual things that happened.

For sure, mention if you wrote any referrals. In fact, leave a copy of the referral for the regular teacher.

Also though, tell about anything surprising that came up in a class discussion. I was watching a Civil Rights Movement documentary with a social studies class once when I heard several students joking with each other, using racial slurs. I was shocked and appalled. The lights were out, and I was in the back of the room where I could watch them all without their knowing which students I had my eyes on. Unfortunately, this meant I couldn't tell which students were speaking.

I stopped the video and made a general announcement that racial slurs were racism, and racism is unacceptable. I felt that their regular teacher should reinforce what I had told the class. I also suspected they would not have said those things had he been present. In my note to him, I simply wrote:

"Several students made racial comments during the documentary. I told them this was racism and that racism is unacceptable."

Note any student questions you were unable to answer.

Obviously, only note for the regular teacher unanswered questions about the material in the regular teacher's lesson plan. She isn't going to care what questions came up in a class discussion on the NBA finals if you started it in order to fill the last five minutes of class time.

Do note if students asked the meaning of something on the assignment sheet, if you didn't have an answer for them. Here are some other questions students have asked that I have noted for the regular teacher:

"Will this be on the test?"

"What are we going to study next?"

"Does my essay have to have quotes?"

When students ask these questions, I explain that their regular teacher will need to answer, but I will make a note of their question. I used to just tell students:

"I don't know that."

I like my current system much better, and I'm sure the students and their regular teachers do, too.

This should go without saying, but never make up an answer just to appear that you know what you are talking about! This causes a lot of harm and not a bit of good. There is no shame at all in admitting:

"I don't know that."

No one knows everything. It is just even better to say:

"I don't know, but I will leave a note for your teacher, and hopefully she will tell you when she gets back."

Attach and explain the student sign-out sheet.

To your note to the regular teacher, attach the sheet you used to keep track of which student was out of the room, like you told the students you were going to. In your note, explain the sign-out sheet to the regular teacher.

You don't know what the regular teacher will do with this information, but the students' reactions when you told them you would be giving this to their teacher should be good indications of what she will do with it. Hopefully, this knowledge kept students from leaving the room unnecessarily.

Leave the regular teacher a way to contact you.

At the end of the day, after all the students have left, put your phone number by your name (or attach your business card), and leave the note in the middle of the teacher's desk — or in her mailbox in the school office, if she shares the classroom.

I have been requested for many repeat assignments. These teachers knew who to request because I paper-clipped my business card to the note I left them. My business card has my picture on it so that teachers can match my name to the face they often see in the halls and in the teacher's lounge. I only substitute at two high schools, so most of the teachers recognize my face.

I have also been called a few times by teachers who could not locate something in their room after I had been there. They were relieved to have my number to be able to ask me about it, and this has also led to them requesting me to substitute for them again.

If you don't have business cards, then at least write your name and number on the note. Some substitutes print up their own personalized stationery. Business cards are better. I often see them sitting in the teacher's top drawer, waiting to remind them of me the next time they plan on being absent. I got my business cards really inexpensively through http://www.vistaprint.com/.

Here is a sample, fictional note to a regular teacher, to give you an idea how a professional one looks:

Monday, May 21, 2012

Substitute: Mrs. Kelley

Hello Mrs. Smith,

Period 1 finished their reading and answered all the questions. Their papers are in the period 1 box. They asked when the quiz will be. I told them you would answer this when you returned to class.

Period 2 prep – I period-subbed for Mr. Green.

Period 3 finished their reading, but we had a lively discussion on why Romeo is so interested in Juliet all of a sudden, when he came to the party to see Rosalyn! I told the class my theory is that "Romeo and Juliet" is a farce about how hasty and irresponsible some teenagers can be. They didn't get the chance to finish answering all the questions in class, so I let them do that for homework and made it due tomorrow.

Period 4 worked on their projects as assigned.

Period 5 took the test as assigned. I set aside Bob Smith's and Joe Brown's papers because Bob was letting Joe copy off his paper.

Period 6 finished their reading and answered all the questions. Their papers are in the period 6 box. I referred Katy Webster to the office because she refused to turn her music down and she would not quit tapping on her desk. The rest of us couldn't concentrate on reading the play until after she left.

Attached is the sign-out sheet students signed, so that you can see who left the room, and why.

(I paper-clip my business card here.)

See how to write these?

I had some negative things to report in this letter, but notice how I just reported on them in a matter-of-fact way, without complaining. I kept it short and to the point without using any unusual abbreviations or slang. The regular teacher knows right where all her classes left off, so she should be able to pick right up where I stopped.

If the regular teacher has been out more than three days and there are more than two other notes from substitute teachers who were there before me, then I staple all the notes together in reverse order, with the newest on top. This is just how I would want it if I returned from a long illness, rather than papers scattered all over my desk.

WHICH HIGH-SCHOOL CLASSES TO SUBSTITUTE TEACH

The substitute coordinator will probably ask you to fill out a form indicating which classes you can substitute teach. The wording on this form varies from school district to school district. Some districts use very strict wording that doesn't give you much choice in which classes you substitute. Other districts leave it all up to you.

Some school districts require actual certification in any subject you substitute teach, the same as for their regular teachers. For these districts, you have no choice but to only indicate which classes you have a credential to teach. This is not as limiting as it sounds. With my English credential, I can teach drama, journalism, and yearbook as well as basic English classes, writing classes, and language-arts electives like public speaking, debate, and desktop publishing.

Most school districts I have subbed for are less stringent on substitute qualifications than they are on regular teacher qualifications. There are two different approaches they take. Some use a form that asks which classes you feel qualified to substitute, while other districts ask what you feel comfortable subbing. These are two distinct questions that require you to consider different things.

Classes you feel qualified to substitute

If the substitute coordinator asks which classes you feel qualified to substitute, then stick to classes you have training or experience in. This does not have to be academic training or teaching experience. If you were a newspaper journalist for twenty years, then you are eminently qualified to substitute in the journalism classes. Your thirty years' experience as a homemaker qualify you to substitute in home economics classes (which are now called family and consumer science classes). If you work out, run, coach, or play sports you will probably be a great physical education (PE) substitute.

There is professional or life experience that could qualify you to substitute teach almost any high-school class. You should only indicate you feel qualified to teach technical classes like math and science if you did well in those classes yourself and remember the material or have self-educated yourself and are up to speed on it, though.

Classes you feel comfortable substitute teaching

This is my favorite type of class choice. It gives me the most leeway to choose classes I will enjoy substitute teaching. Most of the school districts I have chosen to substitute in use this approach. Your comfort zone likely differs from mine. However, you can benefit from knowing the reasoning I use when I fill out the type of form that asks which classes I feel comfortable substitute teaching:

English

English was my undergraduate major, and I love sharing what I know, so I circle all the English and language arts classes.

Arts and Crafts Electives

I circle all the arts and crafts electives like drawing, painting, drama, public speaking, debate, chorus, band, orchestra, computer programming, CAD, graphic arts, sewing, cooking, and flower design. These classes are usually full of students who love what they are doing, and so they are a joy to substitute. The regular teacher will leave a lesson plan that allows these students to work on ongoing projects or review things they have previously learned, so it doesn't matter if you have no expertise in the subject matter. You will be there mostly to make sure they clean up.

Advanced Classes

Advanced classes such as calculus, physics, and anything with AP in front of it (advanced placement in college) are generally full of students who love to learn, and so they are also fun and rewarding to substitute. I circle all these. As with the art classes, the regular teacher leaves the students a project to work on, reading to do, or a test to take. I am there just to supervise students and make sure they use their time wisely.

General Education

General Education classes in math, history, English,

foreign language, and science are usually pretty good on a substitute. The teacher usually leaves review work, a test, an applicable DVD to watch, or a chapter to read and questions for the kids to answer. The only tricky part is getting the DVD to play, which works differently in every classroom. If I want a lot of work, then I circle most of these.

If I have money coming in from freelance work or royalties so that I don't need to substitute as much, then I don't make myself available to substitute in general education or the rest of these classes:

Physical Education (PE)

PE is probably fun to substitute teach if you're an athlete. I'm not though, so it is just a bunch of running around and trying to project my voice outside or in a large gym. PE is really difficult for me, so I avoid it if I can. Sometimes, I show up for history or math and that teacher has one or two PE classes, though. That is another good reason to wear sensible shoes at all times.

Special Education / Resource Room / Special Needs

This sounds more scary than it is, because these classes have para-educators in them. The para-educator is a paid adult instructional aide who is assigned to that classroom and knows the students and their routines. Special Ed / Resource classes are still pretty challenging, though. These are some of the neediest students, and I haven't been trained in how to meet their special needs. I avoid Special Education / Resource Room / Special Needs classes, if possible.

However, just a few weeks ago I accepted an assignment in math and the school office asked me to switch into a resource classroom. They wanted to switch me with the substitute who had been in that math classroom the day before. The school office lady was really puzzled over why the substitute assignment computer had reassigned yesterday's math substitute to be today's resource substitute.

I understood all too well what had happened, but I kept quiet about it. The substitute assignment computer offered the resource assignment to that other substitute and not to me because she had made herself available for resource-room assignments, and I hadn't. The office asked me if I would switch, and I graciously went along with it. It's in my best interests to maintain good relationships with all the school office ladies.

If you do substitute in a class that has a paid adult instructional aid in it, introduce yourself to the aid when you arrive.

Ask him or her:

"Are you a general classroom aid, or are you assigned to a particular student?"

If the paraprofessional aid is assigned to a particular student, then just run the class as you normally would. The aid might be a sign language interpreter for a deaf student, or something similar. He or she really has to pay attention to that one student, and cannot really help you monitor student behavior like a general classroom aid could.

However, if the para-professional is assigned to the whole class, then ask him or her how they would like to divide up duties for the day, much as you would with a student teacher. Remember, as the substitute for the regular teacher, you are still responsible for all the students in there. Do not leave the room except for maybe a minute to use the restroom while the aid remains in the classroom, supervising the students. Pay attention to what is going on.

Sometimes, the aid and the regular teacher will have a routine where they split the students into two groups and each take half, and then switch groups. Work this out with the aid or aids when you first arrive, so that everyone has a clear picture who is doing what. If the aid wants to step in and act as teacher and lead the classes for the day, I let him or her do so and just stay to support. I support by helping individual students with their work and helping them stay on task.

It all goes smoothly so long as before we start, we talk about who is going to do what. And so long as you, the substitute for the regular teacher, remember that you are in charge. Your job and your very teaching license are on the line. You are responsible for whatever happens in the classroom.

My first time subbing in a special education classroom went horribly wrong. I was twenty-something and forgot I was in charge. The aid was 50ish, the age I am now, and I just accepted her authority, based on how much older she was. She told me I was to take this one kid on the bus for an outing for the day, and I naively did it! This kid was a handful! He kept trying to run away from me, and one time he even tried to bite me!

Worse than that, though, I left the aid alone with the other kids in the classroom. I would have been responsible for anything that went wrong in there, and never even known until the report arrived in the mail, firing me and suspending my teaching credentials.

Do not let this happen to you. Remember that when you are subbing for the regular classroom teacher, you are the one in charge of all the aids in the room. They may try and act otherwise, and if they do, put your foot down. Call the office lady for back-up if you need to. She might find another room the aid can go to for the day.

Remedial Classes

Remedial classes that don't have para-educators are the most challenging to substitute in. These students are really needy, and as a substitute who doesn't know them I have faced my toughest challenge. I don't circle any remedial subjects. I also make a point of finding out the names of these teachers so that I can decline these assignments if someone bypasses the list and calls me for them even though I did not sign up to substitute in them.

Shop Classes

I accept shop-class assignments in the school district where I substitute now. The shop teachers here are sane enough to realize no substitute is going to know their shop well enough to run it safely in their absence. They leave a movie for their students to watch, or a chapter for them to read, or drawing-board work for students to do in preparation for future shop work.

However, I have subbed in other districts where shop teachers allowed students to use the shop equipment in their absence. The few times I was in those classes were some of the scariest days of my life! Kids were welding things and using high-powered saws. I am so blessed that none of them lost limbs because I didn't know how to supervise them on the equipment they were using.

Before you make yourself available to substitute shop classes, ask around in the teacher's lounge until you discover the practices of the shop teachers.

THE TEACHERS' LOUNGE

Substitute teaching is one of the loneliest jobs out there, so far as making friends. If you can manage to sit with the same people at lunch each time you are at a particular school, this is one of the few ways to make real friends at this job.

Where teachers sit to eat lunch varies by school. At the school office in the morning, ask the person you check in with if there is a teachers' lunch room, and if so, where it is and if you need a key. Some high schools have a separate teachers' lunch room for each department. Often, it is called a work room. Some high schools have nothing, and teachers congregate in particular classrooms, sometimes including students. Some have separate lounges for adults who are teachers and adults who are non-teachers (classified employees).

Some high schools have so many more students than they were built for that they have to have two or more lunch times. As noted earlier, make sure you know what time your lunch is. Call the office before it comes up, if you are not sure. Lunch time is something the students cannot be trusted to inform you on accurately.

At one school where I substitute often, I always sit with the custodians. Before you find that odd, consider what good connections they are:

Custodians are sort of the Secret Service of the school. They have radios, so they know the lowdown on everything that is going on, and they can relay messages to key places on campus. Custodians have keys to every room in the school. At almost any time, I can find a custodian out in the hallways. More than once, they have helped me out of tight spots.

The custodians at this particular school are all in their 70's, too. Many of them have been at the school their whole adult lives, and graduated from it before that. They are great sources of all kinds of information.

I heartily recommend that you sit down to lunch with regular teachers, if you can find some during your lunch time.

It feels weird at first, but just politely ask if you can sit with them. Say something like:

"May I join you?"

Don't be too pushy, of course, but at a lull in their conversation, ask your burning questions such as:

"What do you do at this school if students are playing with their phones during independent work time in class?"

If the regular teachers seem shocked that you have to ask if students are ever allowed to admit they have cell phones, just explain that schools vary on this and you want to make sure you are doing the right thing for this campus. Explain that at some schools, teachers allow students to listen to music through ear buds during work periods and after they are done with tests. Get their reactions to this so that you know if it is acceptable here.

Do not get involved in the regular teachers' controversial discussions or gossip. Listen politely, but do not offer your own opinion. Tread lightly. Don't take sides. Try to keep yourself open to everyone, not just one clique of teachers.

I am fortunate that my father was a teacher.

Before I started substitute teaching, Dad explained to me that if it seems like the regular teachers are interviewing you right there in the lunch room, they probably are — for potential future substitute-teaching assignments. If you don't realize this is what is going on, then it seems like they are being awfully rude, assuming, and personal in the questions they ask you:

"What area is your certification in?"

"How long do you have left in college?"

"Where did you get your bachelor's?"

"What was your major?"

"Have you done your student teaching?"

"Have you ever been a regular classroom teacher?"

"Do you want your own classroom?"

You want these regular teachers to request you for future substitute-teaching assignments, so be professional. Answer the regular teachers' questions seriously and thoughtfully. If college degrees are required in order to substitute in your state, they will probably ask you what your major was. In states that do not require a bachelor's degree, they might ask about your job experience outside of substitute teaching.

In most cases, the regular teachers are really asking you which classes you are best-qualified to substitute teach.

Explain your qualifications just as you would in a job interview. Ask the regular teachers what they teach, and then tell each one about your experience and education in their subject. I once informed a "consumer and family science" teacher that because I had been a homemaker for 30 years, I felt very qualified to substitute in her home economics classes.

Whatever you do in the teachers' lounge, do not complain.

Other substitutes often come into the teachers' lounge to complain about the students:

“Kids these days!"

"They don't know how to spell!"

"They have such terrible attitudes!"

"You have to work like hell just to get them to sit down!"

"You have to tell them three times just to get their pencils out!"

"They don't know what irony means!"

"They don't know their times tables!"

Do not join in on this, not even if the regular teachers join in on it. Complaining about students might seem like a bonding activity for making friends with the regular teachers, but I have seen it from both sides – as a substitute and as a regular teacher, myself. As a substitute, it feels great to finally get some adult time and talk among adults. You get a false sense of security that tells you it is OK to say what you are really thinking. It is not.

When I was a regular teacher sitting in the teacher's lounge, I always made note of the substitutes who complained – so that I could make sure and exclude them from substituting in my classes. Why? Complaining is a sign of immaturity. Someone who complains is less likely to be able to handle difficult situations when they arise. A regular teacher's biggest concern with having a substitute teacher in her room is:

Will the substitute allow my students to trash my room while I am gone?

Regular teachers request substitutes who seem mature enough to keep everything under control.

Don't be surprised if the regular teachers vent. Do not repeat anything they say.

The teachers' lounge where I currently work is a pleasant place where everyone makes chit chat about the weather and movies and sports. It is actually a staff lounge that includes the custodians, secretaries and lunch ladies as well. I really love it here.

However, I have been in many teachers' lounges that were places where teachers went to vent and let off steam about their frustrations with students and the administration. Do not repeat any of the gossip you hear in there. Leave if it makes you uncomfortable. Nothing will get you ostracized faster than tattling on your peers for things they say rather than do. It is petty to do so in any workplace, not just in teaching.

Don't join in on this complaining, either. See the section above: Whatever you do, do not complain. If this sounds like a double standard, it is. Deal with it. Life is not fair, only games are.

I used to enjoy my teacher privilege of cutting to the front of the school cafeteria lunch line.

When I first started subbing, fresh out of college, I lorded (ladied?) it over the students. Today, I feel rude doing this. More and more, I subscribe to the philosophy that I need to treat students the way I want them to treat me. I feel more and more convinced that the way to earn respect from high-school students is to show them respect. Most of the textbooks on teaching and substituting are written with younger children in mind. You do have to command the respect of younger children. High-school students are almost adults, though. More than anything, they want to be adults. Most of them are old enough to recognize respect when you show it to them, and to respond in kind.

Besides, buying lunch is just too much trouble. I just substitute at two high schools these days, but when I went to many different school campuses it was difficult to keep track of where to go and who to see, in order to buy a "teacher lunch." I would rather bring my lunch and spend more time enjoying it.

These days, I always prepare a lunch the night before a school day, just in case I get called in to substitute. If I know for sure that I will have access to a microwave at all the schools where I might be needed, then this can be as simple as buying frozen dinners that fit in my lunch bag. If access to a microwave is uncertain, then I make a sandwich, or gather some carrot sticks and dip, or make an individual salad. I do keep change in the pocket of my lunch bag, in case there is a bake sale or the cafeteria offers something I really want to try.

Tread lightly on the treats.

If there are treats or lunch items out in the teachers' lounge, and no note saying, "Help Yourself," or anything, I would wait and see if I was invited to partake. Sometimes, this is a potluck, and only people who brought stuff are eating it. Other times, a student club or something has donated the food and everyone is welcome to enjoy it. Don't assume you can eat something just because it is out there. Wait until you are invited, or you at least casually ask a staff employee (not another substitute) what is going on.

People get weird about food. I don't want to stop getting asked to substitute at a school just because of some petty thing with a potluck, so I am careful to not assume I can eat something just because it is out. I always bring my own lunch and just start eating it when I get there. Then, if someone invites me to take some of the food that is out, I might or I might not. I never want to make a mistake and eat someone else's potluck. Besides, I lost 90 pounds last year. Bringing my lunch makes keeping trim easier.

A Substitute Teacher's Status as a Guest

One of the high schools where I currently substitute always has coffee brewed in their "Hospitality Room," for the teachers and other staff. I love this so much that I considered telling the substitute coordinator to only schedule me at this school – until my mom reminded me that then I wouldn't be treated as a guest anymore.

My mom is a registry nurse who is on call at many different hospitals. Our two jobs have enough similarities that we often give each other tips. Mom once consented to only be on-call at one hospital. That was a big mistake. They started to say stuff like:

"You know how we do this."

"You are here every day."

"You know where that is."

"You should know this procedure by now."

In the good schools, one of the few benefits of being a substitute vs. having your own classroom is that substitutes are treated like guests who can't be expected to know how they do things or where everything is. Everyone understands that you travel from school to school. They realize you don't have the bell schedule memorized. They know you don't have a classroom or office where you can leave stuff, so they understand why you carry your lunch around with you in the halls. They are happy to answer even your silliest questions and to show you where to find things you need. Most of the school office personnel I have worked with have even been happy to have the office assistants photocopy things for me, in the schools that are good to substitute teachers.

Anyway, back to the coffee in this one high school's teachers' lounge. I had been drinking the communal coffee all year, with the blessings of all the custodians I sit with, when one of the lunch ladies pointed out there is a coffee club that takes coffee donations from members at the beginning of the year. She implied I should either donate or quit drinking their coffee. Maybe my guest status there is in question, even though I am not there every day. I plan on donating some coffee at the beginning of their next school year.

On "teacher appreciation day" last year, the PTSA brought in little bags full of cookies for all the teachers.

I asked them, "Are those for substitutes, too?"

"Of course! Help yourself!"

I am usually made to feel welcome to whatever treats are available in the teacher's lounge. I have heard from other substitute teachers that they don't always feel welcome to partake in teacher treats at every school where they substitute. While I do believe this is rude, I would remember I was a guest and act accordingly, not insisting on being included. That would be just as rude on my part. I just wouldn't go back to any school that put out treats for teachers but excluded substitutes.

The irony is that the lunch lady who was upset with me for drinking the communal coffee without donating any gets health insurance, and her paychecks from the school district are almost certainly larger than mine. I was tempted to tell her so. I'm glad I held my tongue and was the bigger person. Maturity means taking responsibility for your own feelings and for the way you affect others – even if they don't reciprocate.

As I have been trying to explain throughout this book, the most important quality in any teacher is maturity.

Always be the grown-up in any conversation. Always take the high road. Always be the bigger person. Always do the right thing. Get it?

School holidays and summer vacation are lean times for substitute teachers. We don't get paid unless we work, and we can't work when school is out. What we must never do is allow our bitterness over this to show. I put on a happy face the Friday before Christmas vacation, Easter vacation, and summer vacation. I smile and say to the office lady:

"Have a great summer!"

"See you next year!"

"Enjoy your vacation!"

"Have a great long weekend!"

For ways to truly enjoy non-school days yourself, see my chapter on Money-Making Ideas for Summer and Christmas.

The full-time school employees have an incredible amount of influence over how much you work, as I have explained throughout this book. Don't be a party poop-er, a bring down, or a bummer about their vacations, or they won't want to see your face around their school any more.

I did open my big mouth and tease one of the custodians at our lunch table back when he made a joke about our relative status at the school. I did it in a light-hearted, joking manner that went over fine. I pointed out that he drives a Mercedes, while I had to take the bus home that day because we only have the one truck and my husband worked that afternoon. One of the other custodians chimed in and said, "Yeah, he ought to offer you a ride home!" Everyone at our lunch table laughed, but he didn't offer me a ride home.

A substitute teacher may appear to have the same status as a regular teacher...

A substitute teacher may appear to have the same status as a regular teacher, but make no mistake: we are the lowest school-district employees on the totem pole. The regular teachers, librarian, counselors, lunch ladies, secretaries, custodians, and bus drivers belong at the school. Substitute teachers are guests at best, imposters at worst. Knowing this and owning this is a necessary step to approaching the job with the maturity needed to keep it.

I don't mind the lack of status I enjoy as a substitute teacher at all. I had a salaried job as a claim adjuster at Farmers Insurance for eight years, with lots of status:

- Company car

- Company laptop and cell phone
- Unlimited mobile data plans
- The ability to work from home

Do you know what all that status amounted to? It meant I worked 70 to 80 hours a week with no compensation for overtime, that's what.

The three years I put in as a salaried classroom teacher had similar weekly hours, also with no compensation for overtime. The regular teachers can have the status.

The hours are one aspect in which subbing does not give you a very clear idea what it is like to be a teacher.

Imagine dealing with students all day and then either staying after school three hours or taking three hours' worth of work home with you every day.

But wait, there's more.

On top of that, regular teachers are required to be chaperones at dances, plays, and games — all without any overtime compensation. I've been there and done that. I loved supervising the proms and plays, not so much the games.

Are you having trouble imagining what teachers do after school every day for three hours? They have to plan lessons, grade papers, enter the grades into the grading system or calculate class grades by hand, keep their rooms neat and orderly, meet with parents, attend faculty meetings... Little did I know when I majored in English, the paper-grading workload is highest for high-school English teachers. That makes sense if you think about it: if students write essays, then English teachers have to grade essays.

The regular teachers can have the status. They earn it. Status is not something I crave in life. I relish the guest treatment I get as a substitute, and the chance to interact with students instead of being caught up in grading papers and planning lessons. I love the freedom I have to take a day off whenever I want. I love that I show up at 7:15, leave at 2:45, and don't have to take student papers home with me. I am happy at the bottom of the totem pole. You might not be, but so long as you need this job, I recommend you don't show it.

Don't be overconfident in the teachers' lounge.

While a substitute has to appear confident in front of students, the opposite is true in front of the regular teachers. They respond better if you ask for their help. Regular teachers want you to look up to them, not quite as superiors, but as veterans. It's worth doing so. Even the regular teachers who are much younger than you have a better handle on the culture at this particular school. They make great allies, and formidable enemies. Any regular teacher has the power to make sure you either substitute a lot, or not very much at all.

Too often, new substitute teachers come into the teachers' lounge smugly bragging about how they handled this kid or that situation. Most often, older male substitute teachers are the ones doing this, but younger substitute teachers and female substitute teachers have embarrassed themselves this way, too, and not even realized it.

Bragging has the opposite effect from what you want. Instead of highlighting your achievements, bragging shows how insecure you are. Veteran teachers are unlikely to request a substitute who they perceive is insecure. How is an insecure person going to keep their room intact for them in their absence?

If the idea that bragging shows you are insecure is new to you, you can read more about it at the Mayo Clinic's website under "Narcissistic Personality Disorder."

Get the Scoop on "In-service Days"

Regular teachers often get "in-service days" when the students won't be at school and the teachers receive training: on new technology and new techniques in teaching. Many of the regular teachers take this training for granted at best, and wish they could be in their classrooms planning lessons or grading papers, in the worst cases. You will know these days are coming up because they are on the school district's master calendar, which is usually on the school district's website.

While you are in the lunch room, listen for any hints of what upcoming "in-service days" might be about. If you don't hear anything and the "in-service day" is approaching fast, ask the regular teachers if they know what will be happening on the "in-service day." If they don't know, it is worth asking your friend the office lady to see if she can find out for you.

Unfortunately, school districts rarely think to include substitute teachers in training sessions for new technology. They don't usually think of training substitutes on the state testing practices, either. This cuts out a lot of work you could get. Be a little proactive in letting the office lady know you would like to be included in such training. Perhaps even write or email the principal and ask permission to attend in-service events on your own time or however you want to word it so that the principal knows that you know you will not be paid for attending in-service events. Most school principals will be happy to let you attend training, but you need to be invited and not just show up. That would be awkward.

Also, know that this training will probably not be paid, for you as a substitute. Don't get resentful about that or discuss it with anyone at work. Not having the money in the budget to pay substitute teachers to show up for training is probably why they don't invite substitute teachers to training. Make pay-for-training a non-issue, and you can probably attend all the "in-service" days you want.

Many "in-service days" provide official clock hours of "continuing education" credits, which teachers in most states need in order to renew their teaching credentials. In many states, this applies to substitute teachers, too. If you can get this training for free through the school district, why whine about not getting paid for it?

Some school districts post sign-up sheets for training, and make training mandatory for substitutes to have access to sign in to the computers and the smart boards and the other gadgets that regular teachers like to use in their lesson plans. Ask the office lady if such sign-up sheets exist. Being one of these "technology enabled" substitutes gives you an advantage when it comes to regular teachers requesting you to fill absences.

Regular teachers would much rather have a substitute who knows how to use the gadgets they normally use when they plan their lessons, rather than have to rewrite their plans for a substitute who cannot access those gadgets.

WHEN YOU NEED THE RESTROOM

In newer school buildings, every classroom key should open every staff restroom. Find out ahead of time, and request a staff restroom key if the classroom keys won't open staff restrooms.

Whenever you leave the classroom, make sure all the students leave, too, and then lock the door. You are responsible for everything in the classroom. Don't leave it available for students to wander in there and steal or vandalize.

As a substitute, the worst that could happen would be you not getting invited to substitute at that school again, but that is pretty bad. In nicer neighborhoods, this is usually not a problem, but in tough parts of town you definitely want to lock your classroom door if you leave for even a minute. Err on the safe side until you get a good feel for common practices in each building where you substitute teach.

You legally cannot leave the classroom during class time unless there is another licensed adult in the classroom or you are taking all the students to an alternative classroom such as the library or the computer laboratory. You have to plan your restroom breaks for during the regular teacher's preparation period and your lunch time. Go during these times even if you do not feel the need.

If your classroom is close enough to the staff restroom and you are substitute teaching in a school where teachers commonly leave their classrooms unsupervised during passing periods, then you can sometimes sneak in a quick restroom break then. However, do not be surprised if another teacher beats you to it and the restroom is occupied!

In buildings where it is common practice to lock the room whenever there is no teacher present, you need to limit your intake of coffee (and other liquids) before school and during your breaks. Keep your fluid intake to a minimum before school and during school. Try your hardest to at least wait until passing period to use the restroom, if you cannot wait until lunch or your prep period.

Your prep period might not be free time, either. Realize the office might call or send a student and ask you to cover another teacher's class during your prep period. Include that in your restroom planning. Use the restroom on your way to the other classroom, if possible.

Restroom emergencies do happen. At the high-school level, it is better to rush out for a minute than it would be if you soiled your pants. Always know where the nearest staff restroom is. This is another reason you should have a map of each school you substitute in. If staff restrooms are not on your maps, then find them and draw them in.

In a restroom emergency:

A restroom emergency is when you urgently need to go, right in the middle of class. You are not supposed to leave the students unsupervised. You are legally responsible for them. But you need to go. If your classroom has a door into another classroom, or if your door is right next to another classroom door, call the other teacher over. Quietly explain your emergency and ask if he or she can watch both classes for a minute.

If no other teachers are close enough to watch both classes for a minute, then in an emergency call the office and ask if they can send someone over to give you a restroom break. If you are prone to restroom emergencies, then wear adult diapers. Ladies, it's a good idea to wear a sanitary napkin every day, just in case.

I would never use drugs to suppress the call of nature.

There was a funny commercial on late-night TV for a while. It showed a teacher in front of young students. She got a funny look on her face and you could tell she urgently needed to move her bowels. They played a catchy jingle as she ran to the restroom and back. She took the drugs they were advertising, and then they showed the teacher in front of the students, smiling, no longer in such dire need to leave the room. The jingle was what made it so funny, but jingles are copyrighted, so unfortunately I can't recreate it here.

While I did feel tempted to get the product this commercial was advertising, I know better. I'm not a medical professional, but in my personal, common-sense opinion messing with the mechanism that tells you your bowels need to move is asking for the worst sort of trouble!

I am afraid that if I mess with that mechanism, it will break. Imagine it no longer working. What if you never knew when you were about to have a bowel movement? Not knowing when you needed to urinate could be just as bad.

Nope, inconvenient as that feeling might seem, having that feeling is much preferable to not having it to signal the need to go! No drugs for me, if I can help it. I don't want to take the chance of drugs messing up God's design for my body.

"If it ain't broke, don't fix it!"

WHAT DO SUBSTITUTES DO DURING PREPARATION PERIOD?

A student teacher asked me recently, "What do you do during the regular teacher's preparation period? I thought it was kind of cute. He was earnest, explaining that he photocopied papers for his mentor teacher during prep, and watched him write on the board and enter grades in the computer and call parents and attend meetings. Preparation period is anything but a break, for the regular classroom teacher. He was having genuine difficulty imagining what a substitute teacher would be doing during this time.

This student teacher's question touches on a truth: This job is many things, but I like to say, "It's never boring." Preparation period is the only time it is remotely possible for a high-school substitute teacher to get bored, after using the restroom, that is.

Sometimes, I don't get a preparation period. The school office calls and asks me to cover another teacher's class during preparation period. This is called "period subbing." The school office asks, but really I don't have much of a choice. If I want to be thought of as a team player and keep being requested to substitute at that school, I say, "Yes," and I do it, well, with a few exceptions. Under no circumstances would I agree to substitute in a classroom for severely handicapped students. That requires very specialized training that I am not interested in completing.

Getting along with the ladies in the school office is not a bad thing at all, though. It does work both ways. They know they can count on me to say, "Yes" when they call on me to period substitute. I know I can count on them, too. They have done many little favors for me, from having the office TAs photocopy oral-report score sheets at a moment's notice to giving me excellent job recommendations.

It can get bad.

A middle-school office lady once called and asked me to cover their in-house suspension room during the regular teacher's preparation period. In-house suspension is a classroom where the regular teachers send all the students who don't know how to behave themselves. Rather than reward delinquents by letting them stay home while they are suspended from their normal classroom, they send these kids to "in-house."

Have I mentioned that as a substitute teacher, you have no real authority? Well, you have even less authority as a substitute teacher overseeing in-house suspension. If that happens again, I am saying, “No.”

At the time, I just said, “Yes,” and I did it. It went OK. There was a security guard in the room with me. I told the security guard I would not be back to that school, however. That was just too stressful a situation. What the heck was I going to do if one of those kids started acting up? I didn't even know these kids' names, let alone what all their behavior issues were.

I told some of the regular teachers at the other middle school how this middle school expects substitutes to keep order in the in-house suspension room. They were shocked, so I know this was not just me being oversensitive or work averse.

"They put you in a room with students you didn't even know and expected you to be the ultra-disciplinarian for them?"

"Yep."

"What were you going to do if the students decided to act up?"

"Run."

I did end up returning to that middle school, but not until after it got a new principal. Under his new management, substitute teachers were no longer expected to keep order in the in-house suspension room. By the way, he had been the principal of the other middle school at the time I had spoken with regular teachers there. A proverbial grapevine grows among all of the buildings that belong to a school district, and word does spread. Be aware.

In many states, you must get a lunch break.

I looked up the United States Department of Labor regulations on meal breaks, and they do not require workers to get meal periods. The Federal regulations only state that if you do get a meal period, it does not have to be counted as time that you worked or hours toward the overtime cutoff.

However, many state labor laws do require workers to get meal breaks. Both states where I have worked do: Washington State and California. Check the labor laws in your state.

If your state requires a meal break, then remind the office lady about this if she calls you in to period substitute during your assigned teacher's lunch break.

A high-school substitute teacher who is not asked to period substitute does pretty much anything she wants, during the regular teacher's preparation period.

Elementary schools usually put substitute teachers to work every minute, except while we eat lunch. Regular elementary school teachers have playground duty, hall duty, lunch room duty, bus duty, and doubtless a dozen more duties. They are more than insistent that we substitutes do our fair share of these duties.

A substitute for a high-school teacher pretty much has a break during the regular teacher's preparation period, unless she is asked to period substitute for another teacher. In these tough economic times, another teacher often has class scheduled in her classroom during her preparation period, but she can go to a nearby teachers' office or to the teacher's lounge and read, play with her phone, or chat with other substitutes who are on preparation periods.

Be careful about using school Internet connections during preparation period, even on your own hardware. Read each school district's Internet usage policy carefully. Some don't mind if you use their Internet access for personal business so long as it is not while students are present. Others will fire you over this, as I mentioned in the chapter on what to get from the substitute coordinator. Get their computer and Internet usage policy in written form, and read it carefully.

I like to walk the halls, if I have a free preparation period. This gives me exercise, and it keeps my face in front of many school-district employees. It also helps the school administrators, who are responsible for monitoring the halls. It helps them if I ask wandering students for hall passes, that is.

Of course, if there is not a class in the regular teacher's classroom during her preparation period, then I take this opportunity to leave her classroom in better condition than how I found it. I straighten up the rows of desks, find a spray bottle and a rag and clean the white boards, maybe even clean grime off the student desks and dust the bookshelves.

I know from being a regular teacher myself that the condition of her classroom will be the regular teacher's number one concern, after a day she has a substitute.

As I explained in the chapter on having students keep the room tidy, school budgets are slim these days. Custodians no longer clean student desks, nor dust anything. These tasks are only demeaning if you make them so.

I used to turn the lights off and close the door so that no one would see me straightening the room. (I still do on days when the kids got the best of me and I have to pick sunflower-seed shells out of the carpet.) Most of the time though now, I just smile at whoever came in and talk to them while I clean. Other adults rarely ask me what I am doing. They know the budget situation. If students ask, I just cheerfully explain the desks are grimy. The students usually know this, though.

FIRE DRILLS AND OTHER BUILDING EMERGENCIES

As I mentioned in the chapter on substitute folders, you need a copy of each school's emergency drill plans. You also need the emergency evacuation route for each classroom you substitute in. Get copies of these from the person you check in with in the school office, or find out if they are already in a substitute folder or posted in each classroom.

If there is an evacuation drill, make sure and at least take pen and paper with you so you can take roll at your evacuation site. The best case scenario is if you can take a roll sheet with you. However, with most roll sheets being computerized nowadays this is often not practical at short notice. You can make do with a blank sheet of paper. Have the students line up. Go down the line and have each student print his or her name on your paper.

I still cringe at the memory of one of my fire drills as a regular teacher. I hadn't brought the roll sheet outside with me, and two of my students walked away from the rest of my class. My principal came up to me at the end of the drill, bringing those two students. He was visibly angry. I was responsible for those two students, and I hadn't even noticed they were not with my class.

Line the students up, take roll, and make sure they stay lined up there. Don't let them wander away. You are responsible for them.

There is usually an emergency backpack in the classroom that you are supposed to take with you on these evacuation drills. Take it if you can find where the regular teacher keeps it. Sometimes, you know its location from the lesson plan, the substitute folder, or from some standard procedure for that school building.

There might be a roll sheet for each class period in the backpack, so it is worth taking and checking. It is also supposed to contain bandages, alcohol wipes, other first-aid supplies, water, and other things you might need in an emergency. If you use up any of these supplies, then inform the regular teacher in the note you leave for her.

There are other drills besides evacuation drills. Ahead of time, ask the office for a copy of the school building's emergency procedures, so you can be ready for these. The alarm and procedures are a little bit different, for each kind, and in each school district.

We had a bomb scare.

We had a bomb scare one year when I was a regular teacher. I had only been at this school a month or so, and my colleagues were not very attached to me. I didn't even know what was going on until after all this was over. I was very confused until later when I figured out they had sent me in search of the bomb:

"Go into each classroom in this cluster and look for any

backpacks, bags, or purses that students left behind."

"Here's someone's backpack."

"Run it out into that field."

Just kidding! I didn't find any backpacks or bags or purses, but I often wonder what they would have had me do with any I did find. If I had read the emergency procedures beforehand like I was supposed to, I would have recognized the bomb-scare alarm and cleared out of there the moment I heard it. It was my preparation period, so I didn't have any students assigned to me.

What a patsy I was. This was while I was a regular teacher, trying to get tenure (which I never got). I do not think substitute teachers would be asked to check for bombs, and anyway as a substitute, I'd say, "No."

LONG-TERM SUBSTITUTE TEACHING ASSIGNMENTS

I have completed one long-term substitute-teaching assignment. It was at a middle school, and it was tough. I'll tell you what I learned from this experience, in case it helps you. Long-term subbing is not my thing. It carries just as much responsibility and work as being a regular classroom teacher, at a small fraction of the pay. I didn't get health insurance, either.

Still, if you are trying to get experience and recommendations toward becoming a regular classroom teacher, long-term subbing is a good way to do that. In most school districts, it also will make you a little more money on average than short-term subbing. If you need the money, you should probably accept, if the school district offers you a long-term substitute assignment.

Long-term subbing is not all bad. Some nice things about a long-term substitute assignment come out of knowing where you will be every day, for the term of this assignment. You can pack your lunch with confidence, knowing if there is a microwave in the staff room. You can actually sit with the same people in the lunch room every day and get to know fellow teachers a little. You can learn all your students' names and use names in all your classroom interactions.

I got my long-term substitute assignment because I was "highly qualified" in the subject, according to No Child Left Behind. This meant I was fully credentialed in English and had experience teaching English.

After I completed this one long-term substitute teaching assignment, I was offered many more, but I turned them all down. Each time, I was contacted by a school principal directly, by phone. Unlike normal assignments, they even left detailed voice mail and expected a reply.

The principal and his assistant interviewed me, for the one long-term assignment I did accept. I asked if I could come in along with the regular teacher for a few days, so that she could show me her procedures on passing out books and turning in papers and all the other logistics of how she managed the classroom. I think this is what endeared me to them and got me the job.

"Yes!" they said joyfully, "I'm sure she wants a transition."

They even called the substitute coordinator and arranged for me to be paid for those two transition days.

Back Door to Teaching-Credential Renewal

There is a limit on how many days you can substitute per school year for one teacher in a subject you don't have a teaching credential for specifically. Each state has its own law on this. In California, the limit is 30 days. This worked to my advantage, actually.

My California Single Subject English teaching credential had expired while I adjusted injury claims for Farmers Insurance from 1999 to 2007. I was certified as "highly qualified" per "No Child Left Behind" because of my college English major and experience teaching high-school English. However, I had been hired on an emergency substitute teaching credential to long-term substitute for an English teacher.

The substitute coordinator emailed me after I had been there three weeks and told me about the 30 day rule. My first reaction was anger. "Why didn't she tell me this sooner?" It took all the maturity I could muster to not go off on her in a reply email.

However, I remembered some interesting information I had received from the California Commission on Teacher Credentialing, years before. I mentioned earlier that my California teaching credentials had expired when I moved back to the state after the first time I lived in Washington State. I had written to the Commission and requested an extension on the time I had to renew my credentials, so they wouldn't actually expire, retroactively. The Commission wrote back and told me something interesting.

They like to grant extensions on credential renewal only after you have secured employment with a school district. Yes, this is a Catch 22. How are you supposed to secure employment with a school district without the credential? Well, apparently there is a back door through the substitute coordinator's office at each school district.

When I got that email from the substitute coordinator telling me I had a week to get my extension on renewing my credential or my long-term assignment would end prematurely, this interesting bit of information came into my mind, and I took action based on it.

I forwarded her email to the California Commission on Teacher Credentialing. They renewed my California Single Subject English teaching credential two days later, and my Multiple Subjects for the Self-Contained Classroom credential the day after that, for good measure, I guess.

Without this pressure from a school district needing my services, who knows how long it would have taken the Commission to renew my credential, or what hoops they would have made me jump through. I have heard through the grape vine that this is common among most, if not all, state teacher licensing agencies: they are more likely to license you if your services are already being requested by a school district in their state.

Here is another little secret I can let you in on:

The regular teacher is still getting paid, or there wouldn't be a substitute in the room; they would hire a regular teacher. This means the regular teacher is still the official teacher of record. Her name and reputation are at stake. She should be planning the lessons for you, or at least helping you gather materials.

In exchange, you should be maintaining the regular teacher's procedures on passing out papers, handing in papers, and all that jazz. This way, it will be easier for her when she returns.

Get in writing from the regular teacher what the students need to get accomplished while she is out. In math, this might be "up to page 310 in their textbook." In English, it might be "read Macbeth and write an essay on it." Get a very good idea of what her expectations are, especially if you will be planning the lessons. All states have requirements for what students have to study in each grade in all academic subjects, so if you go too slowly she might have an impossible job of catch-up to do when she returns to the classroom. If this happens, you can kiss goodbye any positive recommendation from her.

The teacher I long-termed for and I had agreed I would be the teacher of record and plan the lessons. However, the district wouldn't go along with this. Because they were paying her anyway, they insisted that she remain the teacher of record, plan the lessons, calculate final grades, and prepare the materials. Planning is my least favorite part of teaching, so this made me very happy. Not all my days were happy, though. Far from it.

Being a long-term substitute teacher is much different from being a daily substitute.

Being a long-term substitute was much different from my normal stint as a one-day substitute. I had some actual authority with the students, because I was grading their work and I was allowed to contact their parents.

I did this largely through a computerized parent contact system, which was actually pretty cool. It allowed me to report to parents on tardy students and those who weren't doing their work, without having to play phone tag with their parents. I just input the codes into the computer, and it kept calling the parents until they answered their phones.

Because I had actual authority with the students, I couldn't play my usual grandmother role.

Usually, I spoil the students and then give them back to their regular teacher. I give them all the attention they want and let them talk as much as they want. In exchange, they cooperate with my reasonable and appropriate requests. Why not? I am only there for the day, usually. What harm could it do?

My "let them talk" policy was a real problem when I was a long-term substitute at the middle school. The outgoing students were constantly talking during work periods, and the quieter students started to complain that they couldn't focus on their work.

It is much easier to make rules at the beginning of a long-term substitute-teaching assignment. Once you have started to spoil the kids, it is very difficult to back pedal and make them be quiet, like a regular teacher would. I don't plan on ever accepting another long-term substitute assignment, but if I did I would lay down the law on my first day, just like a regular teacher. I would insist that students be quiet during individual work periods, and that all talking during group work periods be about the work.

Being a long-term substitute was more like being a foster parent, than like being a grandparent.

The students kept saying they missed their regular teacher. They kept asking when she was going to be back, even though I had explained she would be out for the rest of the school year. This was discouraging. It made me feel like chopped liver.

Now, these were middle-school students. High-school students would probably be a little more mature about this. They might be thinking they missed their regular teacher, but they probably wouldn't tell me.

DON'T BE A BAD EXAMPLE

So far, this book has been about how you should behave. Hopefully, by now you grasp what it takes to be an excellent high-school substitute teacher:

1) Be an adult: Take responsibility for your own success.

2) Model for the students what being an adult looks like.

3) Insist that students take responsibility for their own success and thus behave like adults.

In this chapter, I am going to tell you about some bad examples I have observed, over the years. I am doing this to clarify what it looks like when adults regress into childhood. Don't regress into childhood, at least not in front of any school-district employees, nor in front of any students – nor their parents.

By the way, school-district employees, students, and their parents shop at the stores you shop at, ride the same public transportation, eat at the same restaurants, and go to the same movie theaters. Chances are, some of the students you come into contact with work at these establishments. Pretty much the only place you can ever be sure no work-related person will see you is in your own home – and perhaps in the homes of friends who don't have other friends over or whose children don't have other friends over.

I mentioned before that my dad taught high school for 30 years. He used to really annoy my sister and me by refusing to go to certain restaurants and movie theaters. We thought he was being silly.

The first time I walked into a restaurant on the weekend with a date (before I was married) and saw a student there, I totally forgave my dad for all those times I found him so annoying. It can be fun seeing students outside of school; don't get me wrong. However, you have to always watch what kind of an example you are setting, because you never know when or where you might be setting that example.

Bad Example #1: Temper Tantrum Substitute

I walked into the main school office one busy morning and got in line to check in and get my substitute folder. Suddenly, a man who was older than me threw a temper tantrum! In front of several students who were in the office, not to mention all the office staff, he got up from one of the chairs in the waiting area and started yelling at the school office lady who was checking the substitute teachers in:

"I was here early, but somehow you lost my assignment! Now all these people are coming in after I have been here for ten minutes already, and they are getting paid substitute assignments while I just sit here without one!"

If you think this man will ever get a paid substitute teaching assignment in this district, you are as delusional as he is. He just proved that he cannot be relied upon to behave appropriately in front of the students, nor to model how they should behave in similar situations. He regressed from adulthood – where we take responsibility for ourselves – into childhood, where we expect others to take care of us.

The substitute check-in lady called one of the other ladies over and told her,

"We have a situation here."

Some men in suits came and escorted Temper Tantrum Substitute out of the room.

Even if Temper Tantrum Substitute is friends with a school-board member who pulls strings for him and gets him some substitute-teaching assignments at this school, what do you think is going to happen when Temper Tantrum Substitute calls the school office for back-up? If you don't know what I am talking about, then go back and read the chapter on making friends with the school-office staff.

Even cussing sets a bad example for students. We call them on using profanity, so we had better not be using it, ourselves. Not ever, because habits are hard to break. The short answer is we must control our tempers at all times, and we certainly must not throw temper tantrums.

Bad Example #2: Cigarette Smoking Teacher

When I first started teaching, I smoked cigarettes. That is a filthy and entirely unhealthy habit. Looking back with 20 / 20 hindsight, I don't blame any of the principals or school-board members who didn't hire me because they could smell smoke on my clothes at the job interview.

The fact is: if you are a smoker, your next cigarette always takes up part of your attention. In the back of your mind, even when you aren't smoking right this minute, you are anticipating that next cigarette. It distracts you from important things.

Here is the story of how I quit smoking. If you smoke, use it to help you quit. If that link doesn't work for you, search on Google, Yahoo! or Bing for "Cherise Kelley" AND "How I Quit Smoking".

Back at that high school where they sent me around to check for bombs in backpacks, I used to spend my preparation period in "the smoking lounge." None of the schools in Washington have those. This state's school campuses are 100% smoke-free.

Anyway, there was this other teacher who smoked and had the same prep period as I did. She was coordinating a trip to Europe with about 100 students. Every day for months she was on the phone planning and coordinating — and smoking. One day when I came in there, she looked miserable. The company she had booked the Europe trip with had skipped out with these 100 students' money. I don't know for sure that this would not have happened had she not been distracted with cigarettes, but I wouldn't hire anyone who smokes to do anything for me.

Bad Example #3: Boozing Teacher

When I was in high school, two of my friends had a teacher who hid bottles of liquor all over his classroom. They said he nipped at these bottles from time to time, during class. He seemed to think no one knew about this, but everyone knew. They made fun of him behind his back. I'm sure he would have been fired if he hadn't had tenure.

Movements are afoot to get rid of tenure so that teachers like him who take advantage of tenure to misbehave can be fired. I know that teachers who have tenure are insulted by this. I agree with the way one of the regular teachers at a school where I substitute now put it, though:

"Some teachers forget why we are here. We are here to serve the students."

Parents want us to be good examples to their kids. Wisconsin is just the beginning. The voters' point of view is:

"Why should teachers be guaranteed jobs even when they misbehave? They have a strong influence over minors, so teachers should be held to even higher standards of behavior and morality than the rest of society."

Don't drink on the job.

Don't come to work hung-over or smelling like booze.

If you have a problem with alcohol, Alcoholics Anonymous is in every phone book world-wide. Call and ask when the next local meeting is. Be the very best example you can be to the kids. Don't give their parents a reason to want you removed from their child's school.

Bad Example #4: Obese Teacher

My 7th grade health teacher was obese. She probably weighed 400 pounds. She was a health teacher! She was supposed to teach us about nutrition and exercise and all that is sensible. I don't know for sure if her influence led to my becoming fat later in life, but it couldn't have helped.

Yes, I was a bad example this way, as well. I got overweight while I held a desk job from 1997 - 2007. I didn't lose the weight until 2012, as recorded on my blog, Size 12 by St Patrick's Day. I did lose the weight, though, when I was 49 years old, and I am keeping it off.

- Being fat is a choice.
- Fat is not genetic.
- You are not just "big boned."
- You are capable of being normally sized.
- Choose to be normally sized!

If you have the use of all your limbs and are able to exercise, it is even relatively easy. All I had to do to lose 90 pounds was walk every day for half an hour and limit myself to three sensible meals per day. That's it. Simple. The hardest part was deciding to do it. Once I committed myself to it by telling everyone I knew, the rest was pretty darn easy.

You don't have to join a gym.

You don't have to buy any drugs.

Just buy a raincoat, a snow coat, and some waterproof walking boots, and go for a brisk 30-minute walk every day, no matter what the weather.

I bought "new" used clothes at thrift stores every month, as my size kept changing. In total, losing the weight cost me less than $400, over the course of 10 months. Eminently doable. Getting "new" used clothes every month was even fun; it was an unanticipated joy.

Bad Example #5: Inappropriate Teacher

In one classroom where I recently subbed, the regular teacher had taped to the wall by her computer a poem a student had written to her. I initially thought that was sweet, but then I read the poem.

I won't violate the student's copyright by quoting the poem here. I will just try to convey why it was inappropriate: The poem described the teacher's anatomy in a way that did not suit a minor student's relationship with an adult teacher. It was a rhyming poem. The second-to-last line ended with a harmless word that rhymes with 'pass.' Use your imagination about what the last line should have ended with. It didn't, but it was implied.

Yes, the poem was funny.

Yes, it was complimentary.

No, it was not appropriate.

The teacher should have thanked the student for the compliment and then explained why it was an inappropriate gesture to make to a teacher. The last thing she should have done was tape the poem to the wall for other people to see!

We had a guest speaker in our seminar who was a substitute teacher, when I was in my teacher-training program at San Francisco State. He was a successful substitute, and his gimmick was that he rapped with students. (This was 1990.) A few weeks later, a school principal came to our seminar and told us this substitute had done "something inappropriate" with one of the students, and had been fired. We all wanted to know exactly what the substitute had done, so that we could avoid it. The principal wouldn't tell us, and I still wonder to this day. However, we all know what is inappropriate behavior with minors. We must remember this at all times.

Some of the high-school boys tried to flirt with me, when I was a young substitute. One of them put his arm around me and said, "I think she's fine!" (At the time, that meant I was the bee's knees, the bomb, the cat's pajamas, a fox, or whatever kids say at the moment to mean really good-looking.) Rather than scold him and embarrass him so he lost face in front of his friends, I just joked about it, saying, "You're not my type." I did this in such a way as to brook no more nonsense, though. Thankfully, I am old enough to be past this now. It stopped when I was around 30.

Make it absolutely clear that your interest in the students is pure. Hugs from students are a big panic moment for many substitute teachers. We know our motives are pure, but a casual observer doesn't. Neither do all the people who might see a photo of an innocent hug. A student that a substitute teacher has sent to the office for not doing the work might see such a photo opportunity as his chance to get revenge. This is another reason high-school substitutes need to be low-key and non-confrontational, as I describe in the chapter on how to keep the students from wrecking the classroom, and other horrors.

Each of us has to decide for ourselves ahead of time what we are going to do if a student innocently tries to hug us. My solution is to raise my arms up so that I look like a letter 'T'. I figure that makes it obvious that the student is hugging me and that I am not hugging the student back. You have to sort this out for yourself, but do so before it happens.

Do not take your cue from regular teachers. Their unions protect them from this sort of thing. Most substitutes lack union protection. If we are accused of wrongdoing, we are simply fired and forgotten. Avoid even the appearance of wrongdoing.

A few regular teachers have sent me messages through their students by texting the students. These teachers being familiar enough with the students to have exchanged personal phone numbers so they could text each other is the epitome of inappropriate. Do not exchange personal phone numbers, Facebook addresses, etc. with students.

Remember, students have friends. They need you to remain professionally distanced so that you can be the voice of reason and get them back to work and get them on the right track when they start to misbehave. This is not going to happen if you befriend students.

If you try to be friends with students, you will be locked into their weird rules of what is "cool" and what is not. You will be getting peer pressure from students! This is completely inappropriate and career-destroying, and possibly even scandalous enough to hit the evening news someday. Don't exchange personal phone numbers or email addresses or Facebook addresses with students. Period.

Students have asked me if they can hug me. I say, "You can hug me, but I can't hug you." By high-school age, students understand that I have to be fearful of lawsuits, so they don't get their feelings hurt when I say this. If they decide to hug me anyway, I turn sideways and hold my arms up like I am a big letter T, so it is obvious to any observer that the student is initiating the contact and it is innocent. We are standing side by side with our arms over each other's shoulders for a second, is all.

The lawyer who the university had in to discuss this with us in my education course when I did my student teaching told us not to touch a student if we were doing so for any selfish purpose. This includes if we are having a bad day and need a hug. Don't request this from students. You are there to teach them. He said to only touch them for their good: pull them apart to stop a fight, tap their shoulder to get their attention if they are not responding to your voice.

I don't even do those two. For one thing, I am not paid enough as a substitute to get in the middle of a student fight. I will put my hand on someone's back if I am walking behind them in the halls or the cafeteria, and say,

"Behind you," so that they don't back into me by accident. That is about the extent of it.

It is a careful walk and a thin line, between being appropriate and not being a stick in the mud. Walk that line. You want the students to respect you for the responsible adult that you are, but you don't have to be humorless or plastic. Just be a grown-up among the almost-grown-up, and you will be fine.

Bad Example #6: Bad Ethics Teacher

Every teacher is an ethics teacher, consciously or unconsciously, regardless what subject they theoretically teach. If you think it is OK to lie, cheat, or steal, then the students might start thinking that is OK, too. If you have bad ethics, then do the kids a favor and don't be any kind of teacher. On the off-chance you don't know what I mean by ethics, I'll elaborate:

Show up.

If you accept a substitute teaching assignment, then show up for it. Show up early so you have time to read the lesson plan and get the classroom ready. Show up showered, dressed professionally, sober, with enough sleep the night before, and not smelling like cigarettes.

Only cancel for illness or business reasons. Cancel as soon as you realize you are ill or that you need to be elsewhere for a business reason. If you have the teacher's contact information, let her know you are canceling, so she can make other arrangements.

"Business reasons" include appointments, other jobs, and

being asked to do a long-term or better-paying substitute-teaching assignment in another school district. I would not cancel the morning of the assignment to take a better-paying assignment that same day. I might cancel for a better assignment if I were able to give a day or more notice for them to make other arrangements.

Tell the truth.

Be honest in your note to the regular teacher. If you forgot to follow part of the lesson plan, or if the students behaved badly, then let her know. The students will tell her anyway. Don't make up an answer if a student asks you something you don't know. Shrug and say:

"I don't know that, but I will leave a note for your regular teacher so that maybe she can tell you."

Keep your hands to yourself.

Don't walk off with any school supplies or students' belongings. Don't touch anyone you shouldn't.

Do straighten up and clean up the regular teacher's room before you leave, though. Straighten the rows of desks or neaten up the clusters if they are arranged in groups. Pick up papers off the floor. Put the chairs up if you forgot to tell the students to do so. You are there in place of the regular teacher, and she would be doing this if she were present. She is much more likely to request you to substitute for her again if she returns to a clean, orderly room.

Be nice.

Don't turn teaching into a power trip where you oppress

the students.

For one thing, this will backfire on you as a substitute. Day-to-day substitutes don't have any real authority. You will crash and burn if you behave as if you did.

For another thing, teachers who turn school into a power struggle have forgotten why we're here. School is supposed to benefit students. It is supposed to be their place of learning, not your place of oppressing. Be firm, but nice.

Have standards.

Have standards, for your own behavior as well as students' behavior. Don't allow students to be rude, disrespectful, or mean to each other, nor to you. Call the office lady for back-up if students won't cooperate with your attempts to moderate their behavior.

Don't you be any of those things, either. If you use humor, don't make it at anyone's expense. Laugh with students, not at them. If you are a genuinely nice person, this should all come easily to you.

Do the job you are being paid to do, to the best of your ability.

Don't text or talk on your phone during class. The students are not allowed to do so during class, and you are their role model. Don't just read or surf the Internet. Walk around the room in a random pattern, encouraging students to stay on task. Help students with their work if you are able. Pay attention to them. Watch from the back for cheating if they are taking a test. Do not sit down and rest for more than a few minutes at a time.

Be a mature adult substitute teacher among almost-adult high-school students.

Don't discuss inappropriate topics with students. Remember, they are not quite adults. They are not your peers. You need to maintain a healthy, professional distance from students. Do not discuss your personal life with them.

This is another thing each of us should decide ahead of time: how much personal information to share with students.

I will briefly chit chat about the book I am reading or movies I saw recently. I will answer that I am married, but don't have any children. If they ask me about my religious or political beliefs I will explain them briefly, but only if they ask me. That is it. Any further questioning and I explain it is not appropriate for me to share those details with students.

You have to set your own boundaries, and stick to them. Most of the time, high-school students ask these types of questions to avoid doing their schoolwork. A little chit chat helps you get to know students and is good, but if students persist, asking you personal questions beyond politeness, then remind them what they are supposed to be doing.

Be professional.

Maintain a businesslike environment in the classroom. Don't let it get too noisy or rowdy.

Also, it is unprofessional for teachers to discuss other teachers with the students. Do not do this. If you hear the students discussing teachers, this is OK. They can discuss who gives a lot of homework, who is nice, who they like and don't like, stuff like that. Just don't you participate in it. Do stop students if they say rude things about their teachers.

Do you get the idea?

I could go on and on and tell about teachers who swore, picked their noses, used sarcasm, and other immature and inappropriate behaviors. If you want to do those things, don't be any kind of teacher: substitute or regular. Kids need models of how proper and responsible adults look, talk, smell, and behave. Far too often, their parents are not models of this. God knows the people they see on TV and in the movies are not.

Teachers are the ultimate role models. Teachers need to be the best models of adult behavior we can be. We need to dress, speak, carry ourselves, smell, act, and behave like adults. We simply need to be adults.

AVOID SUBSTITUTE-TEACHER BURNOUT

It's easy to get burned out, as a substitute teacher. You have to work really hard. You never know where you will be from one day to the next. You can get into a rut of wearing old clothes and drab accessories so that you never look your best. It can seem like you are a second-class citizen in the schools, compared with the regular teachers, the teacher's aids, the office staff, and the custodians. You don't get very much pay. Most substitute teachers don't get health insurance or any other benefits. My advice is the same, regardless if you are subbing for money, experience, or joy:

Don't let substitute teaching be your only source of income.

I talk about other income sources in the next chapter. Use as many of these other sources as you can. You won't burn out so fast if you have relief. I substitute for the joy of it, but even so, I only want to substitute two days a week. I substitute more during the busy times when the substitute coordinator really needs me: just before Christmas, in the late-winter cold-and-flu season, and at the end of the school year.

Figure out what age kids you work with best, and stick to that grade level.

Starting out, I wanted to maximize the chances I would work each day, so I signed up for kindergarten through grade 12 (K-12). I also didn't yet know which age-group I worked with best. However, I stayed with elementary school much longer than I should have. I also stayed open to middle school much longer than was prudent. I work best with older teens. I belong at the high-school level. Perhaps it is because I am not a parent, but whatever the reason, I am much happier since I specified "high school only" when I signed up with my most recent substitute coordinator.

Have a good attitude.

You create your own work environment, to a certain extent. Yes, some schools have policies and procedures that are annoying for substitute teachers. Yes, some schools are in rough neighborhoods where the students are more difficult than in richer neighborhoods. However, your attitude can still make or break your experience at these schools.

I have tried this both ways.

I am not just making this up.

Don't learn this the hard way like I did.

On the one hand, if you are upbeat and friendly, then you are more likely to have positive interactions with the people you work with. People you have positive interactions with are more likely to want to help you with any problems you have on the job. Students you have been friendly to are more likely to cooperate with you. Don't misunderstand. I say be friendly, not a pushover. Say "No" to students when merited, but say it politely.

On the other hand, if you are a smug or arrogant know-it-all or whiner, then your interactions with students and regular teachers are more likely to be negative. Can you see why that would be the case? No one feels like helping you with a problem if you always come off like you know everything. Students find you unapproachable when you are like that. No one wants to deal with a whiner any more than they have to, either.

Smile.

Make chit chat.

Say, "Have a nice long weekend!"

Say this even though a long weekend means you won't work, which means less income for you.

Make friends at the schools.

I have mentioned this in other chapters, but it bears repeating. Make friends with the office staff. Only call them if:

1) You need back-up, or

2) Something is preventing you from doing your job.

Call with these two issues as soon as possible, to give the office staff the best chance of helping you.

Go see the office staff during your lunch or during the

regular teacher's preparation period, if it is not urgent enough to warrant a phone call. An example would be if you want an invitation to the next "in-service day" for training at the school. When you go see the office staff, smile at them and then wait patiently while they write down the message they just took from their last phone call. Don't start speaking until they ask if they can help you.

Sit with the same people in the lunch room if you can, each time you go to a particular school. Don't be pushy. Listen more than you talk. Think of the regular teachers as veterans who can teach you about the culture at this school, if nothing else. Teachers like to teach. Let them teach you the ins and outs of their particular school, which includes such things as if teachers generally let kids eat in class or use iPods or cell phones after they finish their work.

Buy your substitute-teaching clothes at thrift stores so you can replace them more often.

Most people understand why you don't wear brand-new nice clothes for substitute teaching. Even high schools have art and PE classes where your clothes have a high chance of getting ruined. Kids will be kids, and the chances of ink stains from errant pens are high. Kids rough house, and your clothes might get torn.

This doesn't mean you have to wear the same old outfits over and over again for years, though. Doing this will cause you to burn out because your confidence in how you look will start to wane.

If you shop at thrift stores for subbing clothes, then you can have three or four outfits that are new to you every few months for the whole school year — all for the cost of just one actual new outfit from a department store. Most of the clothes at thrift stores where I go are barely used, either. People just wore the clothes a few times and got tired of them, from the looks of it.

Heh, or since I mostly buy preppy stuff for subbing, maybe someone's aunt Matilda gave them this sweater vest, and they took it directly to The Good Will Store. It works for me!

Listen to your own feelings about substitute teaching.

Subbing is only fun if you like doing it. You have to do it to see if you like it. Once you have done it, there is no shame in admitting something you have tried is not your cup of tea. In fact, you will be much happier once you admit that and start to move on.

Subbing at the high-school level is very different from subbing at the elementary level. Try elementary if you haven't. You will need a different substitute teaching guide for elementary school, though, one that explains discipline plans.

If you would prefer to have your own classes or to feel like you belong someplace instead of always being a guest, then you are not going to enjoy subbing for more than a year or two. That is enough time to get the experience you need out of subbing. After that, look for another job to do while you try and get a teaching position. Or, go into business for yourself in the meantime, grading papers for individual teachers or something.

If all you want out of subbing is the money, then don't stay on as a substitute past a year or two, either. Nothing burns you out more than subbing, if you don't truly want to be doing it. It is not a bad way to support yourself while you look for something else, but if you don't enjoy subbing, then by all means start looking for something else as soon as you realize this.

Do not wait until you are burned out on subbing to start looking for another job. By then, you may have burned your bridges and ended up with no one willing to give you a good job recommendation.

If you want a regular teaching position at a school, then don't substitute there for more than a year.

Once you are seen for too long as one type of employee, it can be difficult to break out of that pigeonhole. I have heard from more than one substitute that they feel the schools where they substitute like them so much as a substitute that they wouldn't want to lose them as a substitute, and so they wouldn't hire them on as a regular teacher. Regular teachers have told me they felt this way where they were subbing, and so they applied with other school districts to get their regular positions. This pigeonholing phenomenon exists in other industries, too.

For these reasons, if you start to feel like you would love to be a regular teacher at one of the schools where you currently substitute, then let everyone there know that, but stop subbing there after the current school year. One school year is not too long, but if you substitute at a school too long, the general consensus among the teachers and substitute teachers I have discussed this with is they do start thinking of you as a substitute and not a regular teacher.

If the school is in a large school district, then you can probably keep subbing for other schools in the district, just not the one where you want a regular teaching position. Look for other sources of income until a position opens up there, and then apply for it. This is a little like not sleeping with your spouse until that ring is on your finger. Same idea. Don't give away the milk, or they won't buy the cow. Play a little hard to get.

Do keep in touch with the school where you want to be a regular teacher.

Be the office staff's friend and the students' "rah rah" person. They are much more likely to want their friend teaching there than some stranger. Make sure you are a friend, but not a stalker. Don't overdo it. Only show up once every few weeks. Check the district's job postings several times every day, though.

Go to your choice school's plays and their games (but not their dances).

Stop in afternoon with goodies for the office staff a few days before each holiday and vacation.

Let them know how great you are doing but how much you miss them. If anyone asks why you don't substitute there anymore, just level with them. Let them know you really really want to be a regular teacher there, so you don't want to be thought of as a substitute, not by the students nor the staff. Make sure and give them your contact information. Give them a resume only if they ask for one. Just a business card is good until then.

Date, but don't move in until you're married.

Do accept if they offer you a long-term substitute (LTS) position at the school where you want to be a regular teacher, with some cautions.

I know this is kind of like moving in before you are married, but the analogy is not an exact one. Long-term substitute teachers get more respect than day-to-day substitutes. An LTS position is kind of like a paid internship. If you like the school and want to teach there, then go for it.

However, find out why the regular teacher is out, if they don't tell you. If she is having a baby, great. There is nothing to worry about. However, if she is retiring, then only accept one semester as a long-term substitute. After that, if they don't post the position and hire you on as a regular teacher, don't keep subbing in that position long-term.

Yes, this happens. I knew one guy who had been a long-term substitute in the same position for six years. Substitute teachers get hired on as long-term substitutes for regular teachers who are never coming back, instead of getting regular teaching assignments. Don't let them do this to you.

You need to be available to accept a regular contracted position if one comes available. Besides, it is really true that if you don't respect yourself, nobody else will respect you, either.

If they don't hire you on as a contracted, salaried teacher after you have already fulfilled one or at most two long-term substitute jobs, then look for something else full-time with benefits to do until you get your own classroom.

Especially don't stay on as a long-term substitute if they passed you over and hired someone else. You can always go back to daily subbing if you are not able to find something else full-time with benefits, but at least do your best to look for something else.

To re-iterate the key points on not getting burned out on substitute teaching:

- If you would rather have your own classroom, then subbing will burn you out after a year or two.
- A year of subbing is enough experience.
- If you substitute for more than a year or two, then you start to pigeon-hole yourself.
- If you need to support yourself until you get your own classroom, then start looking earnestly for a full-time job with benefits in some other field after you have subbed for a year.
- Don't keep subbing just to show you really want to be a teacher. This almost always backfires and locks you in

as a substitute.

- Keep in touch with your friends in the office at schools where you would love to teach. Make sure they know you want to teach there, but that you find substituting depressing, so you are working full-time at X company. Ask often if they would please let you know of any job openings at their school.

- Keep yourself known to the students at the school where you want to teach by going to the school's games and plays, but not their dances.

More tips for substitute teachers who want their own classrooms:

Carry a copy of your resume with you.

Whenever you are at a school or the district office or a school board meeting, or on any school-district property, there is the possibility you will encounter a school principal who asks to see your resume. Sure, you can make arrangements to send it to him or her, but right there in the moment, he or she really wants to hire you, or you would not have been asked for your resume. Have one ready to hand to any principal who asks for it.

Every moment that you are in a classroom, assume the principal (or the superintendent or a school board member) could walk in.

Always be doing what you are supposed to be doing: supervising the students. You can read if the students are quietly working or reading silently, but stand in the back of the room and read, so that the students cannot see when you are reading and when you are checking on them. Don't sit for more than a minute. Only sit if you need to rest, and if you are sitting, be watching the students.

If a regular teaching position is what you want, then think of every subbing assignment you take as an audition for a regular teaching position.

Give each and every assignment your very best. Other teachers are watching you, too, not just the principals, superintendents, and school-board members. Be someone the other teachers would love to work with, and make sure they know your name and your certification, but without being pushy. Maybe you will get recommended next time a regular teaching position opens up in your subject area in the district.

MONEY-MAKING IDEAS FOR SUMMER AND CHRISTMAS

Substitute teaching is not a full-time job. Even if you substitute every day during the school year, you don't work in the summer or over Christmas vacation. It can be tough to make a living at it, especially in districts that only pay substitute teachers minimum wage. Most substitute teachers have to buy their own health insurance, unless they are covered by their spouse's insurance. Teachers who substitute every day burn out faster, too. You will almost certainly need to supplement your substitute-teaching income, especially in the summer.

Artistic Expression

On days when I don't substitute teach, I write. I wrote this book, and I plan to write more books. I also have written articles for several websites, both through online portals such as "Yahoo! Contributor Network" and for private clients who have their own websites. My cousin sells her hand-made pottery at craft shows. I have a friend who sells homemade incense and bath salts at craft shows. Substitute teaching is the best part-time job for writers and other artists, in my opinion. Days when I don't get called in to substitute are "spoken for."

Freelance Work

My dad was a regular teacher, not a substitute. He had the option to spread out his pay throughout the year so that he got a paycheck every month, but in the beginning of his career he opted for higher paychecks during the school year and no pay over the summer. He painted houses over the summer. He got customers by putting fliers up at supermarkets and paying us kids to put fliers on windshields in parking lots.

In the same way my dad got house-painting customers for summer, you could get:

- Gardening customers
- Errand-running customers
- Students to tutor over the summer
- Old folks to tutor on how to use their cell phones...

Really, the possibilities for being self-employed as a freelancer or consultant are endless. You might have to get a business license. Check at your state's website and your city's website, or at your local city hall.

Mystery Shopping

Through mystery shopping, I have made hundreds of dollars, been compensated for dozens of restaurant meals, gotten hundreds of dollars in free groceries, and have seen dozens of free movies in theaters.

Mystery shopping is busiest in summer, which also happens to be when substitute teachers need work in the worst way. It is freelance work that you do as an independent contractor. Your clients are marketing firms that send you to stores, restaurants, and movie-theaters to covertly check on how good their customer service is.

You patronize the establishment covertly, and you save the receipt to get reimbursed and to prove you were there. You get to keep what you buy. You fill out an online report and some also make you mail in the original report and receipts.

Some marketing firms also offer non-covert assignments such as auditing and merchandising. Market Force does.

Many scam companies promise you mystery shopping work. You can avoid the scammers by never paying anyone money to sign up as a mystery shopper. Some reputable companies I have done mystery shopping for are:

Market Force:

http://www.marketforce.com/

JM Ridgeway:

https://jmr-shoppers.jmridgway.com/

Second to None:

https://apply.second-to-none.com/

Temporary Employment Agencies

Temporary employment agencies have served me well in the past, for summer work. I usually opted for reception temporary assignments, which meant answering phones and greeting clients. There are temporary employment agencies for all manner of work though, from construction to supermarket stocking to dental assisting and nursing.

To find the reputable temp agencies, I would look in that old-fashioned thing no one ever seems to use anymore: the phone book. Other places you can check to see if a temporary employment agency is legitimate are your city's chamber of commerce and better business bureau.

Retail

Retailers always need extra help at Christmas time. They usually are hiring at every store in the mall plus at every other retail store in your town around the beginning of November. An employee discount is an added perk to a retail job. They need the most help the week before Christmas and the week after Christmas. Coincidentally, you happen to be off school those two weeks!

Summer is the slow time for retail stores, though, and all their school-age help is off, too, so retailers are not a good source of summer work.

THANK YOU

Thank you for reading this book. If it helped you, then I hope you will please leave a favorable review at Amazon.com. Favorable reviews there help me sell more books. To find this book's page at Amazon.com quickly: In any search engine's search box, type:

Amazon Cherise Kelley High School Substitute

Made in the USA
Las Vegas, NV
24 January 2023